D0012914

FRANÇOIS-MARIE ... name of VOLTAIRE, was the son of a notary and educated at a Jesuit school in Paris. His father wanted him to study the law, but the young man was determined on a literary career. He gained an introduction to the intellectual life of Paris, and soon won a reputation as a writer of satires and odes – a not altogether enviable reputation, for the suspicion of having written a satire on the Regent procured him a term of six months' imprisonment in the Bastille. On his release, his first tragedy, *Oedipe*, was performed (1718) in Paris with great success; and soon after he published the poem he had written in prison, a national epic, *La Henriade* (1724), which placed him with Homer and Virgil in the eyes of his contemporaries. After a second term of imprisonment in the Bastille, Voltaire spent three years (1726–9) in England, and returned to France full of enthusiasm for the intellectual activity and the more tolerant form of government he found in this country. His enthusiasm and his indictment of the French system of government are expressed in his *Letters on England* (1733), whose sale was absolutely forbidden in France. He is one of the greatest and most universally known figures in all French literature – poet, dramatist, historian, philosopher and writer of masterpieces of fiction such as *Candide*, as well as his widely read *Philosophic Dictionary*. Throughout his life he never ceased from conducting his energetic attack against all manifestations of tyranny and persecution by a privileged orthodoxy in Church and State. He died at the age of eighty-four, after a triumphant visit to the Paris from which he had been exiled for so long.

LEONARD TANCOCK has spent most of his life in or near London, exceptions being a year as a student in Paris, most of the 1939–45 war in Wales, and three periods in American universities as visiting professor. He is a Fellow of University College, London, and was formerly Reader in French at the university. Since preparing his first Penguin Classic in 1949, he has been intensely interested in the problems of translation, about which he has written, lectured and broadcast, and which he believes is an art rather than a science. His numerous translations for the Penguin Classics include Zola's *Germinal*, *Thérèse Raquin*, *The Debacle*, *L'Assommoir* and *La Bête Humaine*; Diderot's *The Nun*, *Rameau's Nephew* and *D'Alembert's Dream*; Maupassant's *Pierre and Jean*; Marivaux's *Up From the Country*; Constant's *Adolphe*; Prévost's *Manon Lescaut* and La Rochefoucauld's *Maxims*.

VOLTAIRE

LETTERS ON ENGLAND

TRANSLATED
WITH AN INTRODUCTION
BY
LEONARD TANCOCK

PENGUIN BOOKS

Penguin Books Ltd, Harmondsworth, Middlesex, England
Penguin Books, 625 Madison Avenue, New York, New York 10022, U.S.A.
Penguin Books Australia Ltd, Ringwood, Victoria, Australia
Penguin Books Canada Ltd, 2801 John Street, Markham, Ontario, Canada L3R 1B4
Penguin Books (N.Z.) Ltd, 182–190 Wairau Road, Auckland 10, New Zealand

—

This translation first published in 1980

—

Copyright © Leonard Tancock, 1980
All rights reserved

—

Set, printed and bound in Great Britain by
Cox & Wyman Ltd, Reading
Set in Monotype Garamond

CONTENTS

INTRODUCTION

VOLTAIRE (François-Marie Arouet, 1694–1778) is probably
the last great writer in Western history with any claim to universal scope. In his day he was admired all over Europe as a
poet and dramatist (tastes have changed, of course), and there
is a span of sixty years between his first tragedy, *Oedipe*, produced in 1718 and his last, *Irène*, at the production of which in
Paris the frail old man of eighty-four witnessed the crowning
of his bust on the stage; the excitement of this apotheosis no
doubt helped to hasten his death a few weeks later. He was a
scientist and philosopher of more than amateur competence, a
distinguished historian, the first in France to lift history from
the level of chronicles of kings and battles, or one-sided propaganda exercises such as Bossuet's *Histoire universelle*. He was a
supreme master of prose fiction, whose philosophical tales,
such as *Zadig* and *Candide*, have never been equalled. A deadly
satirist and polemicist, he was yet full of compassion and
practical kindness towards victims of injustice, cruelty or ill-
fortune. In the midst of all this he found time to keep up the
most voluminous correspondence ever known, not merely in
his own country but with people all over Europe. And for
clarity, lightness and simplicity his prose style is unique. For the
last twenty or thirty years of his long life he was revered throughout Europe as the monarch of letters, and every distinguished
traveller made a point of calling at his house at Ferney, near
Geneva (though it is said that soon after Boswell's arrival
Voltaire found he had a cold and was confined to his room).

The story, partly mythological, surrounding Voltaire's
Lettres philosophiques (here called *Letters on England*) is well
known. The young writer, already notorious for satirical poems
and lampoons of all kinds, was publicly insulted by the

7

Chevalier de Rohan. He committed the social impudence of challenging an aristocrat to a duel. The Chevalier, too grand to accept such a challenge, set his servants on to him to beat him up, and Voltaire, to escape the Bastille or worse, fled to England with the connivance of the authorities, arriving in London in early May 1726. He stayed in England, apart from one quick dash to France for business reasons, for the best part of three years, and what he saw, heard and read changed his life (so goes the legend). He had left a land of slavery, intolerance and darkness and he found one of freedom, tolerance and enlightenment. He had left a virtually feudal civilization in which the people had no say, and any independent thought was subversive; where the Catholic Church was totally intolerant; in which artists, scientists and men of letters were treated as domestics and, without patronage or independent means, had no hope of success. He found a country enjoying religious tolerance (relative, of course), political freedom and democracy (limited by modern standards), with enlightened views on science and philosophy. Literary men were listened to, artists were honoured. He wrote down his impressions in these *Letters*, published in 1734, well after his return to France, an English version, *Letters concerning the English Nation by M. de Voltaire*, having appeared in London in 1733. The book outraged the French authorities, who rightly saw in it a wholesale criticism of the French system, and its printing was forbidden in France. The fuss caused by its appearance sent Voltaire on his travels again. He deemed it prudent to live in Lorraine, and indeed for most of the rest of his life he lived very near some frontier over which he could skip into safety at the first sign of trouble.

The truth about Voltaire's conversion into an admirer of things English is less dramatic and more complicated, as real life usually is. The rarest thing in the world is sudden conversion without any predisposition or preparation; more often people find what they have already been looking for. Which may help to answer the question: Why go to England? Why not cross a simple land frontier into the Low Countries or one of the German states? French was almost a second language there, and in Holland the business of publishing French books, especially those held to be subversive, had already gone on for generations.

The answer is that for a long time before 1726 Voltaire had been intensely interested in English thought and institutions, and had admired much in England's civilization which appealed to the practical side of his character. Throughout Voltaire's thought there runs, like a recurring *Leitmotiv*, his dislike and mistrust of the purely theoretical edifice of unsupported reasoning so characteristic of the French genius, and his preference for practical proof, demonstration, application. A theory is valueless until experiment proves its truth. Hence his mistrust, for example, of Descartes, with his carefully constructed edifice of pure reason, and preference for Locke, who observes the development of a child through the impressions of the material world registered by its five senses. Hence his profound admiration for Newton who, when he found that his calculations did not tally with the then known measurements of the earth, promptly abandoned his calculations until those measurements could be properly established. This is the Voltaire who will say thirty years later with his Candide: *il faut cultiver son jardin*, which might very loosely be rendered: abandoning philosophical hot air, we must each get on with the practical job that lies to hand.

Moreover, this admiration for England is found in his writings well before his sojourn in England. In his epic poem *La Henriade*, on Henri IV, first published in 1724, there is more than one passage extolling Elizabethan England, its practical success, its trade and prosperity.

But there was a personal influence of the first importance. Bolingbroke, the great Tory politician under Queen Anne, having compromised himself with the Jacobites, retired to France at the advent of George I and stayed there from 1714 until 1723. There he married, as his second wife, the Marquise de Villette and kept open house in a château not far from Paris. It was here that Voltaire was a frequent visitor and from this source that he imbibed much of his knowledge and opinions about England. After his arrival in this country Voltaire renewed the acquaintance at the Bolingbroke home near Uxbridge.

Throughout his career Voltaire was an astute business man – indeed he managed his affairs so well that he became one of the wealthiest of all writers before modern times, when copyright, serial rights and properly organized royalties have made literary success financially rewarding. It is not therefore to be wondered at that, in addition to these other inducements to live in England (not unlike the attractions of the United States to Europeans early this century), he was influenced by the chance of publishing *La Henriade* in a good, luxurious edition in London instead of having to rely on clandestine printing and publication, as had been the case in France. To this end, and to make his stay in England useful, he set to work very seriously to perfect his English. How else to understand our literature and get information from the famous people he met? Remarkably soon he was able to write, in October 1726, a letter to his friend Thieriot in very passable English. So he put this to good account by publishing at the end of 1727 *An Essay upon Epick Poetry*, a historical review of the epic genre, including Milton (to flatter his English readers), designed clearly as a boost for his forthcoming *Henriade* which was published in March 1728 and astutely dedicated to the Queen of England. Everything was grist to his mill.

During his stay of nearly three years Voltaire was constantly on the move in London or visiting country houses, ceaselessly talking to representative people, picking up information. He renewed contact with Bolingbroke, he lived for some months at the home in Wandsworth, then an outlying village, of Everard Fawkener (or Falkener), a wealthy business man whom he had met in Paris in 1725. He did not allow his devotion to Bolingbroke to prevent his frequenting Walpole and the Whig hierarchy, for they were now in power. He met the distinguished writers of the day, John Gay, Pope, whose guest he was at Twickenham, saw Swift on one of the Dean's absences from Dublin and established a correspondence with him, Samuel Clarke and many others. He met Congreve, knew theatrical figures such as Colley Cibber, admired the art of the actress Mrs Oldfield (mentioned in Letter 23), was in London at the time of the run of the *Beggar's Opera*, was a frequent member of the audience at Drury Lane, where he saw productions of Shakespeare. Since he mentions the star singers Senesino and Cuzzoni (Letter 23) it is a fair guess that he went to the Handel operas at the Haymarket. He was presented at Court and patronized by Queen Caroline who, like all good Germans at that time, spoke French; and, perhaps most significant of all, witnessed in April 1727 the state funeral in Westminster Abbey of Isaac Newton, a mere scientist, at which the highest in the land were proud to act as pall-bearers.

Given all these demonstrations of English freedom, tolerance and the liveliness of English thought, and the fact that the obvious intention of the *Letters* was to attack the French system by holding up the English model, it would not have been surprising if Voltaire had overdone the merits and virtues of England. So many since, when criticizing their own country, have held up some other as a flawless Utopia. Voltaire never. He is wise enough to moderate his idolatry and flatter the French with some timely bubble-prickings, ironical references to faults, shortcomings or comical quirks of the English, sensing rightly that to hold up the English as perfect would merely put the French reader off. Throughout his career Voltaire was an expert at sugaring the pill. So we are shown, for instance, the funny side of the Quakers, the dreary, life-denying gloom of the Presbyterians. Nor, in the midst of a hymn of praise to the religious tolerance of the English, does he omit to mention that of course nobody's religion is allowed to interfere with the important business of the City and Stock Exchange. Our political system of a limited, constitutional monarchy may be preferable to French despotism, but there is no harm in waxing merry over the antics of the House of Commons. The enlightenment of the English in introducing vaccination for smallpox, then one of the major scourges of mankind, may be admirable, but it is as well to point out that the practice, brought back from Turkey by Lady Mary Wortley

Montagu, only became common after the Princess of Wales, later Queen Caroline, had tried it on her own children, when it immediately became fashionable. For all their anti-French propaganda the *Letters* are almost as much a satire on the English.

All this explains the curious composition of the book and some of its omissions. The French reader in search of information about English life, manners and customs, would find nothing except accounts of various religious sects, a sketchy treatment of our political system, the famous letter on vaccination for smallpox, long and fairly detailed studies of our science, with particular reference to Newton, whom Voltaire rightly hails as one of the greatest geniuses the world had so far seen, a perfunctory study of our literature and cultural life (but nothing on music, painting or architecture) and finally the examination of some of the *Pensées* of Pascal which has no obvious connection with the rest. Not a word about the buildings or streets of London or the grand country houses in which he frequently stayed. The only two architectural features in London that he mentions are Westminster Abbey, because Newton's funeral was there, and the Monument, because he attended a Quaker meeting near by. And, of course, nothing about the English way of life – food, clothing, amusements. Here Voltaire is very much of his age, but he will evolve later with the century and bring touches of local colour into his plays and his tales.

Popular legend, especially outside France, has portrayed Voltaire as the eternal mocker, even a sort of grinning atheist. Nothing could be further from the truth. At least one full-length book has been written about Voltaire's religion. He was haunted by religion all his life, but religion does not imply accepting involved theology or subscribing to ridiculous dogmas. To Voltaire it simply meant leading a good and useful life (practical again) in the hope that there is at last some ultimate justice in the universe. As he expressed it in a famous line: 'If God did not exist, he would have to be invented.' His attitude towards religion, very simplified, may be expressed as follows:

a man's religion is his own honest views about the universe and the possible existence of a supernatural agency. His views are his business *and nobody else's*. Given that it is equally impossible to prove by reason either that God exists or that He does not, nobody whatsoever has any right to dictate what another man believes or whether he believes at all. Any intellectual system which says: 'I am right and all the others are wrong', automatically disqualifies itself. Any dogma claiming exclusive possession of the truth is intolerant of other equally well- or ill-founded views. Intolerance is one of the unforgivable sins in Voltaire's eyes, the others being injustice and cruelty. Now, a religious system which reinforces its intellectual intolerance by denying human rights to those who disagree, by persecution, torture or even death, is not merely indefensible but evil. Hence Voltaire's implacable, lifelong opposition to the Catholic Church. But this raises a question: How far can tolerance go without becoming lazy permissiveness? Where is the point at which tolerance itself becomes evil? How does Voltaire's anti-Catholicism square with the famous remark attributed to him: 'I hate your opinions, but I would die to defend your right to express them.'? Was Voltaire himself being intolerant? But how can a man tolerate a system committed to destroying him? The same dilemma is posed by some political systems today.

It was from this point of view that he looked at the various manifestations of organized religion in England (and by England he means the United Kingdom). The acid test of tolerance is applied once again. The established Anglican Church is ruled out not merely by the scandalously wealthy and slothful lives of many of its priests at that time, but because it denies university education and therefore closes most of the learned professions to non-Anglicans. The Presbyterians are morally intolerant as well as ridiculous because they ban as sinful most of the things that make social life civilized, the innocent pleasures that make life worth living.

This is why Voltaire is so attracted by the Quakers, with their simple, undogmatic cult of spiritual and moral values, the good life, unselfishness and kindness. But although he admires them more than any other sect (ever practical, he judges by the visible effect of their religion upon their lives), he cannot help seeing the comic side of their behaviour. To wear funny clothes and funny hats, to 'thee-thou' everybody, to refuse to take legal oaths, in a word to advertise that they are different, a people apart, is, in Voltaire's view, vanity, however harmless.

Voltaire deliberately blurs the frontiers between Arianism, Socinianism and Anti-Trinitarianism probably in order to show that English Unitarians, or indeed all monotheists, amount to the same thing and have widespread support all over Europe, if not the world. But he regrets that this belief, supported as he claims by the finest intellects in England, Locke, Newton, Samuel Clarke, can never have much popular appeal because it is purely intellectual and its adherents have no wish to make proselytes.

Voltaire's review of the state of religion in England was very ill-served by events. Within about five years of the publication of his attack on the corruption and intolerance of the Anglican Church, perfectly true at that moment, two ordained priests of that Church, John and Charles Wesley, led a nationwide revival of pure Christianity, and a new sect, Methodism, came into being to complicate his rather simple story.

It is a typically Voltairean trick to add a dose of propaganda to everything – he was an inspired journalist. So he tacks on to these letters about England a critical consideration of some *Pensées* of Pascal, with no immediately obvious connection. Two of the dominant themes of his writing will always be horror at the suffering inflicted upon mankind throughout the ages by religious bigotry and sectarian disputes, and hostility to any form of puritanical austerity which aims to suppress the arts, the beautiful things, the pleasant occupations that make the joy of life. Life is to be enjoyed, and the only sanctions should be against enjoyments that hurt or imperil our fellow men. Now, Pascal was the spokesman of Jansenism, the austere puritanical movement within the Catholic Church, which, moreover, subscribed to the Calvinist doctrine of predestination, that is, the terrible belief that only a tiny minority of us is chosen by grace for salvation, and then only on condition that those elect must by their lives and actions deserve it. The rest of mankind, whatever it does and however virtuously it lives, is doomed to everlasting hell. Against this warped view of a good, loving and just God Voltaire recoiled with horror. On the other hand the supreme intelligence of Pascal, who was a great scientist, and his position as master of some of the most eloquent, spell-binding prose in the French language compelled Voltaire's admiration and led to a sort of love-hate relationship with Pascal that lasted all his life. It was this emotional spell of Pascal that Voltaire felt he must struggle against, and the resemblance between some of the more frightening *Pensées* and the dreary and cruel ideas of some British Nonconformists justifies this long appendix.

In politics and economics the tale is similar and needs far less elaboration here. Voltaire admires the progressive liberation of the English, since Magna Carta, from the despotism of King and Church, the gradual development of equality before the law, and above all the system of taxation, however rudimentary it may seem to us compared with the complexity of modern times, whereby nobody is exempt from tax. The inequity of the tax system in France was a scandal which was to be one of the causes of the Revolution, for the aristocracy and the higher clergy were exempt, which of course meant that not only trade and commerce, the real sources of wealth and always respected in England, but also the working people and peasants were crushed beneath the burden of taxation, while the drones and spendthrifts went scot free. But Voltaire had no illusions about the virtues of the 'natural man'. He was much too near the seventeenth century, and also far too clear an observer of human kind, to be taken in by such naïveté. The dictatorship of the mob was to be an invention of Rousseau, or that was what the mob read into him. Years later, when the natural man became fashionable, Voltaire was to write one of his greatest stories about him. *L'Ingénu*, a Huron, drops straight from his prairies into eighteenth-century France and behaves as a natural man, to the consternation of all but a few prurient ladies who see in him the possibility of a new thrill.

Important though religious freedom and political liberalism might be to him, the most significant part of these *Letters*, and the part which was to exert a decisive influence upon eighteenth-century France, was the change of values due to his discovery of English philosophical thought and scientific knowledge. The letters on Bacon, Locke and Newton are the most serious and technical in the book. Bacon and Locke are hailed as great, practical thinkers whose empirical approach freed scientific thought from the fogs of speculation, metaphysics, *a priori* assumptions, and brought it into the light of observed, experimental reality. For a little book purporting to be notes on aspects of English life and thought, the chapters on Newton are remarkably detailed and epoch-making as popular expositions of Newtonian physics, that is to say of science, that remained valid for nearly two centuries. He expounds with a clarity that renders them comprehensible to non-scientists such things as the theory of attraction, optics, astronomy, the reform of chronology and the calculus. He was of course to return to a more detailed exposition of this in his *Éléments de la physique de Newton*, published in 1738, only four years later.

In any work, but above all in a work of propaganda, it is valuable to look for the omissions and ask oneself what rule, deliberate falsehood, guile or mere obtuseness explains the selective character of the data used. The omissions from these *Letters* are extremely suggestive, and the reasons for them fairly clear. His preoccupation with religion and the variety of sects would lead us to expect some mention of the important rôle of the English Freethinkers, especially as Voltaire himself could not accept dogmatic religion. Indeed the position of Toland, Collins, Tindal and the rest ought to have appealed strongly to Voltaire, for they merely demanded that belief in any religious theory must depend upon reason. The omission is all the more surprising since he devotes a chapter to what he calls Socinians, and welcomes the unitarianism he ascribes to such eminent thinkers as Newton and, he claims, Locke. One can only conclude that here Voltaire was being prudent in the knowledge that the inclusion of all this would cause his book to be condemned out of hand.

But it is in the letters on English literature that Voltaire is at his most selective. To begin with, the section on literature is the most perfunctory in the book, often consisting of a page or two of generalities for a whole genre or some important authors. Some of the omissions, however, are so glaring that they cannot be due to mere sketchiness, but must have a reason. The most obvious, perhaps, is *Gulliver's Travels*. We know he admired Swift and especially Swift's great satire. It can only be that *Gulliver*, with its ferocious exposure of so many faults and idiocies of the English, would undermine all his carefully constructed edifice of England as the land of tolerance, democracy and humane civilization. Equally surprising is the omission of Milton from his study of poetry, especially as he had recently discussed him in his *Essay upon Epick Poetry*. Of course the puritanism of Milton was foreign to all Voltaire's instincts, but to omit *Paradise Lost* while making room for people like Waller or Rochester does seem a little one-sided. It is true that Voltaire was the first Frenchman to make an effort to see something in Shakespeare, several of whose plays he saw performed at Drury Lane. He even saw genius in Shakespeare while condemning him as wholly lacking in taste, moderation, observance of the 'rules' and in fact all the qualities of the French classical theatre. He does, however, show some shrewdness when he remarks that the very success of Shakespeare on the stage has inhibited initiative ever since, as writers have thought him beyond praise and therefore simply imitated him. A similar thing was to happen to English music in the eighteenth century, when Handel was deemed incomparable and the only model to imitate. But it is sad to see Voltaire acclaiming Addison's *Cato* as the *ne plus ultra* of the English theatre.

The truth of the matter is that Voltaire came at the most Frenchified moment of our literature, at least since Anglo-Norman times, and his informants all belonged to that way of thinking. The compatriot of Corneille, Molière, Racine and

Boileau felt quite at home with Dryden, Congreve, Addison and Pope, though he did find Wycherley somewhat strong meat. It is a pity that Voltaire was only interested in poetical or dramatic literature, for the great prose writers (unless scientific or philosophical) seem to have passed him by. Not only is no prose of Swift discussed, but he spent three years in the land of Bunyan and Defoe without apparently having heard of them. Less surprising, given his French upbringing (and he was Parisian into the bargain) and the English circles in which he moved, but none the less serious a case of blindness, is that he never even noticed that the English, at any rate since Chaucer, have carried on a love-affair with nature. Love is not blind, and the English have always had eyes for flowers, trees, skies, seasons, beasts and birds, described them accurately and called them by their proper names. Not even the most bewigged classicism could resist this national instinct, and it is ironical that at the very time when Voltaire was in England Thomson was publishing his *Seasons*, which was to have an immense influence upon the revival of interest in nature in France.

This little book contains the seed of so much of Voltaire's later thought and was one of the most influential books of the century upon social, economic and political thinking. By its radical change of values and attitudes it may be said to be a purely intellectual ingredient in the mixture that was to explode some sixty years later in the French Revolution, though had he lived to see it Voltaire would have deplored it as an outbreak of unreason, intolerance and violence bringing civilized human beings down to the level of animals.

But he did live to see one development which was far from his mind when he wrote it. By helping to make English things fashionable he threw open the door to the cult of English sentimentality, the immense influence of Richardson (translated into French by the Abbé Prévost), the stock Englishman in fiction (such as Milord Édouard in Rousseau's *La Nouvelle Héloïs*), *le jardin anglais*, picturesque ruins, 'Gothick' horrors; in a word the whole apparatus of pre-Romanticism.

Voltaire tinkered with his texts all through his life. Passages were suppressed, added and sometimes lifted from one work and published again in another. This makes the selection of the 'right' text very hazardous, and it is unwise to use any of the complete editions of his works.

But fortunately in this case the work of deciding on a definitive text has been done by Gustave Lanson in his masterly edition (*Lettres philosophiques*, Société des Textes Français Modernes, Hachette, 2 vols, 1915). Lanson uses the first French edition of 1734, published, in spite of the name Amsterdam on the title-page, by Jore in Rouen. The Lanson text is followed by Raymond Naves (Classiques Garnier, 1951) which I have used as a working text. The text in the Pléiade edition (1961) also follows Lanson, but it has at least one very serious misreading.

The number of books on Voltaire, even in English, is of course considerable. Theodore Besterman: *Voltaire* (Longmans, 1969) is the fullest biography, extremely interesting to read, with many letters of Voltaire, as one would expect from the editor of Voltaire's correspondence, but it contains a lot of what must be called gossip, however amusing, and is less helpful on the purely literary and critical side. Those looking for good, short, general appreciations in English are advised to read two earlier books: Richard Aldington: *Voltaire* (G. Routledge & Sons, 1925) and H. N. Brailsford: *Voltaire* (Home University Library, Butterworth, 1935). Their age has not lessened their interest as critical assessments.

I am indebted to a most interesting full-page article in *The Times* (22 April 1978) entitled 'Voltaire in London', by Dr Norma Perry, of the University of Exeter.

It would be quite unfair not to mention how much I have owed to my wife throughout the preparation of this translation.

October 1978   L.W.T.

LETTERS ON ENGLAND

LETTER I

*

ON THE QUAKERS

I THOUGHT that the doctrine and history of such unusual people were worthy of the curiosity of a reasonable man. In order to learn about them I went and made the acquaintance of one of the best known Quakers in England who, having been in trade for thirty years, had managed to keep his wealth and desires within bounds and had retired to a country estate near London. I went to unearth him in his retreat; it was a small country house with every amenity but no luxury. The Quaker was a hale and hearty old man who had never been ill because he had never known passions or intemperance; never in my life have I seen a more dignified or more charming manner than his. Like all those of his religion he was dressed in a coat with no pleats at the sides and no buttons on pockets or sleeves, and was wearing a big hat with a flat brim like our clergy do. He kept his hat on while receiving me and moved towards me without even the slightest bow, but there was more politeness in the frank, kindly expression on his face than there is in the custom of placing one leg behind the other and holding in one's hand what is meant for covering one's head. 'Friend,' he said, 'I see thou art a stranger; if I can be of any use to thee thou hast but to say so.' 'Sir,' I said, bending my body and sliding one foot towards him as our custom is, 'I flatter myself that my natural curiosity will not displease you and that you will be so kind as to do me the honour of telling me about your religion.' 'Thy countrymen,' he replied, 'do too much bowing and scraping, but so far I have never seen one with as much curiosity. Come in and let us eat together first.' I paid a few more feeble compliments because we don't shed our habits all of a sudden, and after a healthy and frugal repast which began and ended with a prayer to God, I began to question my friend.

I started with the question that good Catholics have more than once asked Huguenots: 'My dear Sir, have you been baptized?' 'No,' answered the Quaker, 'and neither have my fellow Friends.' 'What? Good God!' I went on, 'so you are not Christians?' 'My son,' he gently expostulated, 'do not swear. We are Christians and try to be good Christians, but we do not think Christianity consists in throwing cold water on somebody's head, with a pinch of salt.' 'God Almighty!' I said, outraged by this impiety, 'have you forgotten that Jesus Christ was baptized by John?' 'Friend, once again, no swear-words, please,' said the gentle Quaker. 'Christ did receive baptism from John, but He never baptized anyone. We are not disciples of John but of Christ.' 'Alas,' I said, 'you really would be burnt in a country with the Inquisition, poor man! For the love of God, let me baptize you and make you a Christian!' 'If that were all we needed to do in deference to thy weakness we would do it willingly,' he went on gravely. 'We do not condemn anybody for using the ceremony of baptism, but we believe that those who profess a religion that is entirely holy and spiritual should abstain as much as they can from Jewish ceremonies.' 'Well, this is something quite new!' I cried. 'Jewish ceremonies?' 'Yes, my son,' he went on, 'and so Jewish that to this day many Jews sometimes employ John's baptism. Look into ancient lore: it will tell thee that John merely revived this practice, which was in use among the Hebrews long before his time, as the pilgrimage to Mecca was among the Ishmaelites. Jesus was willing to receive baptism from John just as he had submitted to circumcision, but both circumcision and washing with water should be abolished by the Baptism of Christ, that baptism of the spirit and cleansing of the soul which saves mankind. This John the forerunner said: *I indeed baptize you with water unto repentance, but he that cometh after me is mightier than I, whose shoes I am not worthy to bear: he shall baptize you with the Holy Ghost, and with fire.*[1] Also the great Apostle to the Gentiles, Paul, writes to the Corinthians: *Christ sent me not to baptize, but to preach the Gospel.*[2] And so that same Paul only ever baptized two people with water, and then it was against his wishes. He circumcised his disciple Timothy, and the other apostles also circumcised any who desired it. Art thou circumcised?' he added. I replied that I had not that honour. 'Very well,' he said. 'Friend, thou art a Christian without being circumcised, and I am one without being baptized.'

That is how our saintly man rather speciously manipulated three or four passages of Holy Writ which seemed to favour his sect, but with the best faith in the world he forgot a hundred that destroyed it. I took care not to argue with him about it, there is nothing to be gained with a zealot; you don't point out to a man the flaws of his mistress, nor to a litigant the weakness of his case, nor reasons to a fanatic, so I passed on to other matters. 'Concerning Communion,' I asked, 'how do you treat it?' 'We do not,' he said. 'What, no Communion?' 'None but that of hearts.' Then he quoted more Scriptures. He preached me a very fine sermon against Communion and spoke in inspired tones to prove to me that all the sacraments were of human invention and that the word sacrament was not to be found once in the Gospel. 'Forgive my ignorance,' he said. 'I have not given thee a hundredth part of the proofs of my religion, but thou canst see them in the exposition by Robert Barclay: it is one of the finest books ever to have come from the hand of man. Our enemies agree that it is very dangerous, and that proves how reasonable it is.' I promised to read this book, and my Quaker thought I was already converted.

Then he explained to me in a few words a few special features that lay this sect open to the scorn of others. 'Admit,' he said, 'that thou hast had great difficulty in preventing thyself from laughing when I acknowledged all thy civilities with my hat on my head and by thou-ing thee. Yet thou seemst too well educated to be ignorant of the fact that in the time of Christ no nation fell into the absurdity of substituting the plural for the singular. They said to Caesar Augustus: *I love thee, I beg thee, I thank thee*; he did not even allow anyone to call him Sir – *Dominus*. It was only much later that men took it into their heads to have themselves addressed as *you* instead of *thou*, as if they were double, and to usurp the impertinent titles of *Lord-ship, Eminence, Holiness*, which worms give other worms, assuring them that with a profound respect and infamous false-hood they are their most humble and most obedient servants. It is to be more on our guard against this base traffic in lies and flatteries that we say *thou* to kings and cobblers alike, never bow to anybody, having nothing but charity towards men and respect for the laws.

'We also wear slightly different clothes from other men so that this may be a constant reminder not to resemble them. Others wear the badges of their dignities, but we those of Christian humility. We eschew gatherings for pleasure, theatri-cal performances, gambling, for we should be greatly to be pitied if we filled with these trumpery things hearts in which God should dwell. We swear no oaths, not even in a court of law, for we think that the name of the Most High must not be prosti-tuted in the miserable wranglings of men. When we have to appear before magistrates over the affairs of others (for we never go to law ourselves), we affirm the truth by a *yea* or *nay*, and the judges believe it on our simple word, whilst so many Christians perjure themselves on the Gospel. We never go to war, not because we fear death – on the contrary we bless the moment which unites us with the Being of Beings – but because we are neither wolves, tigers nor bloodhounds, but men and Christians. Our God, who has bidden us love our enemies and suffer without murmuring, undoubtedly does not wish us to cross the sea to go and slaughter our brothers just because some murderers dressed in red, with a two-foot-high bonnet, enrol citizens by making a noise with two little sticks on a tightly stretched ass's skin. And when, after battles have been won, the whole of London blazes with illuminations, the sky is alight with rockets, the air resounds with the sound of thanksgivings, bells, organs and cannon, we groan in silence over the murders that cause this public rejoicing.'

ON THE QUAKERS

SUCH, roughly, was the conversation I had with this remarkable man, but I was still more surprised when on the following Sunday he took me to the Quaker Meeting. They have several Meeting Houses in London and the one I went to is near the famous pillar they call the Monument. They were already assembled when I went in with my guide. There were about four hundred men in the church and three hundred women: the women hid their faces behind their fans, the men were wearing their broad hats, all were seated, all were profoundly silent. I went through the midst of them without a single one looking up at me. This silence lasted a quarter of an hour. Eventually one of them rose, doffed his hat, and after making a few faces and fetching a few sighs he recited, half through his mouth and half through his nose, a rigmarole taken from the Gospels, or so he believed, of which neither he nor anyone else understood a word. When this contortionist had finished his fine monologue and the assembly had broken up, edified and quite baffled, I asked my friend why the wiser among them put up with such silliness. 'We have to tolerate it,' he said, 'because we cannot tell whether a man who rises to speak will be inspired by the spirit or by folly. When in doubt we listen patiently to it all and even let women speak. Two or three of our devout women often become inspired at the same time, and then there is a fine old rumpus in the House of the Lord.' 'So you have no priests?' I asked. 'No, my friend,' said the Quaker, 'and we are all the better for it. God forbid that we should dare to order somebody to receive the Holy Spirit on Sunday to the exclusion of the rest of the faithful. Heaven be praised, we are the only people in the world who have no priests. Wouldst thou wish to deny us such a happy privilege? Why should we abandon our children to mercenary nurses when we have our own milk to give them? These mercenaries would soon dominate the household and oppress mother and child. God said: *Freely ye have received, freely give*. After such a message shall we haggle about the Gospel, sell the Holy Ghost and turn an assembly of Christians into a shop? We don't give money to men dressed in black to help our poor, bury our dead or preach to the faithful. These holy duties are too precious to be shifted on to others.'

'But how can you be sure,' I insisted, 'whether it is the Spirit of God who inspires you to speak?' 'Whosoever,' he said, 'prays to God to enlighten him and proclaims the Gospel truths he feels, let him be sure that God is inspiring him.' Then he smothered me with scriptural quotations which proved, according to him, that there is no Christianity without immediate revelation, and he added these remarkable words: 'When thou movest one of thy limbs, is it thine own strength that moves it? Doubtless not, for that limb often makes involuntary movements. So it is He who created thy body who moves this body of clay. And the ideas thy soul receives, dost thou conceive them? Even less, for they come in spite of thee. So it is the Creator of thy soul who gives thee thine ideas, but as He has left thy heart its freedom He gives thy mind the ideas thy heart deserves. Thou livest in God, thine acts and thoughts are in Him, thou hast but to open thine eyes to this light which lightens all men, then thou shalt see the truth and make it seen.' 'Oh, but that's Father Malebranche pure and simple!'³ I exclaimed. 'I know thy Malebranche,' he said, 'he was a bit of a Quaker, but not enough.' These are the most important things I learned touching the doctrine of the Quakers. In the next letter you will have their history, which you will find even more singular than their doctrine.

LETTER 3

*

ON THE QUAKERS

You have already seen that the Quakers date from Jesus Christ who, according to them, was the first Quaker. Religion, they say, was corrupted almost from the day of His death and remained in that state of corruption for about sixteen hundred years, but there were always a few Quakers hidden in the world who took care to keep alight the sacred flame which had been extinguished everywhere else until at last this light shone forth from England in the year 1642.

It was at the time when three or four sects were tearing Great Britain asunder with civil wars undertaken in the name of God, that a certain George Fox[4] of the county of Leicester, son of a silk weaver, took it into his head to preach like a true apostle, so he claimed, that is to say without being able to read or write. He was a young man of twenty-five, of blameless life and devoutly mad. Clad in leather from head to foot he went from village to village crying against war and the clergy. Had he only preached against men of war he would have had nought to fear, but he attacked churchmen, and was soon put in prison. He was taken before the Justice of the Peace in Derby. Fox appeared before the Justice with his leather cap on his head. A sergeant gave him a good box on the ears and said: 'You oaf, don't you know you must appear bareheaded in front of the Justice?' Fox turned his other cheek and asked the sergeant to be so kind as to give him another blow for the love of God. The Derby Justice wanted him to take the oath before being questioned. 'My friend,' said he to the Justice, 'thou shouldst know that I never take the name of God in vain.' The Justice, seeing this man thee-thouing him, sent him to the Derby madhouse to be whipped. George Fox went, praising God, to the lunatic asylum, where they didn't fail to carry out the Justice's sentence with full rigour. Those who inflicted the punishment of whipping on him were amazed when he begged them to give him a few extra strokes of the rod for the good of his soul. These gentlemen needed no persuading, and Fox got his double dose, for which he most heartily thanked them. He began to preach to them. At first they laughed, then they listened and, as religious fervour is a catching disease, many were convinced, and those who had scourged him became his first disciples.

Set free from prison he roamed round the country with a dozen proselytes, always preaching against the clergy and being whipped now and again. One day in the pillory he harangued all the people with so much force that he converted some fifty listeners and got the rest so much on his side that the mob pulled him out of the hole where he was pinned, went and hunted out the Anglican parson through whose influence Fox had been condemned to this punishment, and pilloried him in his place.

He even dared to convert some of Cromwell's soldiers, who gave up the profession of arms and refused to take the oath. Cromwell had no use for a sect that would not fight, just as Sixtus V did not think much of a sect *dove non si chiavava*. He used his power to persecute these newcomers; the prisons were full of them. But persecutions hardly ever fail to make converts, and they came out of prison strengthened in their beliefs and followed by their gaolers whom they had converted. But this is what contributed most of all to the spread of the sect. Fox believed himself to be inspired. Consequently he felt obliged to speak in a manner different from the rest of men. He took to trembling, going in for contortions and making faces, holding his breath and then expelling it violently; the Priestess of Delphi could not have done better. In a short time inspiration became quite a habit of his and soon it was hardly in his power to speak in any other way. That was the first gift he passed on to his disciples. In all good faith they copied all their master's grimaces; they trembled with all their might at the moment of inspiration. Hence the name *Quakers*, which means *tremblers*. The small fry thought it fun to imitate them. They trembled, talked through their noses, had convulsions and believed they had the Holy Ghost. A few miracles were needed; miracles were worked.

The patriarch Fox said publicly to a Justice of the Peace in the presence of a vast assembly: 'Friend, take care! God will soon punish thee for persecuting the Saints.' This justice was a drunkard who consumed daily too much bad beer and brandy; he died of apoplexy two days later as it happened, just after he had signed an order sending some Quakers to prison. This sudden death was not attributed to his intemperance; everybody regarded it as the effect of the prediction of the man of God.

This death made more Quakers than a thousand sermons and as many convulsions could have done. Cromwell, seeing their numbers increasing daily, wanted to attract them to his party; he offered them money, but they were incorruptible, and he said one day that this religion was the only one against which he had been unable to prevail with guineas.

They were persecuted at times under Charles II, not for their religion but for their refusal to pay tithes to the clergy, for thou-ing magistrates and refusing to take the oaths prescribed by law.

Finally Robert Barclay,[5] a Scot, presented to the King in 1675 his *Apology for the Quakers*, as good a work as could be. The Dedicatory Epistle to Charles II contains not fawning flatteries but daring truths and good advice.

'Thou hast tasted,' he says to Charles at the end of this Epistle, 'sweetness and bitterness, prosperity and the direst misfortunes, thou hast been expelled from the lands over which thou reignest, thou hast felt the weight of oppression and must know how the oppressor is hateful in the sight of God and men. If after so many afflictions and blessings thy heart were hardened and forgot the God who remembered thee in thy misfortunes, thy crime would be greater and thy condemnation more terrible. Instead, therefore, of heeding the flatterers of thy court, listen to the voice of thy conscience which will never flatter. I am thy faithful friend and subject, Barclay.'

What is more astonishing, this letter, written to a king by an obscure private person, had its effect and the persecution ceased.

LETTER 4

*

ON THE QUAKERS

AT about this time there appeared the illustrious William Penn, who established the power of the Quakers in America and would have made them respected in Europe if men could respect virtue beneath ridiculous appearances. He was the only son of Sir William Penn,[6] Vice-Admiral of England and favourite of the Duke of York, later James II.

At the age of fifteen William Penn[7] met a Quaker at Oxford, where he was a student. This Quaker converted him, and the young man, keen and naturally eloquent, and who had dignity in his appearance and manners, soon won over some of his companions. He gradually established a Society of Young Quakers who met in his rooms, so that he was head of a sect at the age of sixteen.

Having left college and returned home to his father the Vice-Admiral, instead of falling on his knees before him and begging for his blessing, as is the English custom, he went up to him, hat on head, and said: 'I am very glad, friend, to see thee in good health.' The Admiral thought his son had gone out of his mind, but soon perceived that he was a Quaker. He had recourse to every means human prudence can use to urge him to live like everybody else, but the young man only answered by exhorting his father to become a Quaker himself.

At length the father gave way to the extent of not asking for anything except that he keep his hat under his arm when he went to see the King and the Duke of York and refrain from thee-thouing them. William replied that his conscience would not allow that, and his father in indignation and despair turned him out of his house. The young Penn thanked God that he was already suffering for His cause, and went and preached in the City, where he made many converts.

The preachings of the ministers spread more light every day, and as Penn was young, handsome and well set-up, the women of the court and of the town flocked devoutly to hear him. Drawn by his reputation the patriarch George Fox came from a remote part of England to see him, and together they resolved to go on missions to foreign parts. They embarked for Holland, having left a goodly number of workers to tend the vineyard in London. Their labours in Amsterdam met with success, but what did them the greatest honour and most endangered their humility was the reception accorded them by Elizabeth, Princess Palatine and aunt of George I, King of England, a woman noted for intelligence and wisdom, to whom Descartes had dedicated his novel about philosophy.

She was then in retirement in The Hague, where she saw these Friends, for that is what Quakers were then called in Holland. She had several discussions with them, they often preached at her home, and if they did not make a perfect Quakeress out of her, they did at least admit that she was not far from the Kingdom of Heaven.

The Friends sowed in Germany too, but reaped little. The fashion of thee-thouing did not appeal in a country where you always have to have the terms Highness and Excellency on your lips. Penn soon returned to England because of news of his father's illness; he arrived in time for his dying breath. The Vice-Admiral made his peace with him and lovingly embraced him although he had a different faith. William exhorted him in vain to refuse the Sacrament and die a Quaker, and the old man recommended William to have buttons on his sleeves and put braid on his hat, but in vain.

William inherited great wealth, some of which was Crown debts for advances made by the Vice-Admiral during maritime expeditions. Nothing was less secure then than money owed by the King; Penn was obliged to go and thee-thou Charles II and his ministers more than once for payment. In 1680 the government gave him, in lieu of cash, the ownership and sovereignty over a province in America south of Maryland,[8] so now a Quaker had become a ruler. He sailed away for his new state with two vessels full of Quaker followers. Thenceforth the country was called *Pennsylvania* from the name *Penn*. He founded the city of *Philadelphia*, which is now very prosperous. He began by coming to an understanding with the natives round about. It is the only treaty between these people and Christians which has never been sworn to and never broken. The new ruler was also legislator for Pennsylvania; he brought in some very wise laws, not one of which has been changed since. The first is not to maltreat anyone because of his religion and to regard all who believe in any God as brothers.

He had hardly set up his government before quite a number of business men in America came and settled in this colony. The natives of the country, instead of fleeing into the forests, gradually got used to the peaceful Quakers: they loved these newcomers as much as they hated the other Christian conquerors and destroyers of America. In a short time many of these so-called savages, charmed by the gentleness of their neighbours, flocked to beg William Penn to admit them as his vassals. This was a really novel spectacle: a ruler whom everyone addressed as *thou*, to whom they spoke wearing their hats, a government without priests, a people without weapons, citizens all equal, except the judiciary, and neighbours without jealousy.

William Penn could congratulate himself on having established on earth the golden age so often talked about, and which has probably only ever existed in Pennsylvania. After the death of Charles II he returned to England in connection with the affairs of his new country. King James, who had liked his father, felt the same affection for the son, and no longer looked upon him as a member of an obscure sect but as a very great man. In this the King's policy was in line with his inclinations; he wanted to flatter the Quakers by abolishing the laws against Nonconformists so as to be able to introduce the Catholic religion under cover of this freedom. Every sect in England recognized the trap – they always unite against Catholicism, their common enemy. But Penn did not think it necessary to give up his principles to help the Protestants who hated him against a king who loved him. He had established freedom of conscience in America and had no wish to seem to want to destroy it in Europe. So he remained loyal to James II and hence was widely accused of being a Jesuit. This calumny hurt him considerably: he was obliged to justify himself in print. Meanwhile James II, who like almost all the Stuarts was a mixture of greatness and weakness, and who like them did too much and too little, lost his kingdom, though nobody could say how that came about.

All the English sects welcomed from William III and his Parliament the same freedom they had refused to have from the hands of James. It was then that the Quakers began to enjoy by law all the privileges they possess today. Having at last seen his sect securely established in the land of his birth Penn went back to Pennsylvania. His own people and the Indians welcomed him with tears of joy like a father come home to see his children. All the laws had been religiously observed during his absence, which had never happened with any legislator before him. He stayed in Philadelphia for some years and finally left unwillingly to obtain in London some new commercial advantages in favour of the Pennsylvanians. From then onwards he lived in London, into extreme old age, considered as head of a people and a religion. He did not die until 1718.

The ownership and government of Pennsylvania was retained by his descendants, and they sold the government to the King for £12,000. The state of the King's affairs only allowed him to hand over £1,000. A French reader will perhaps think that the Ministry paid the rest in promises and held permanently on to the government. Not at all; the Crown having failed to meet payment of the full sum by the stated time, the contract was declared null and void and the Penn family took back its rights.

I cannot guess what the fate of the Quaker religion will be in America, but I see that it is steadily languishing in London. In any country the dominant religion, so long as it does not persecute, ends by swallowing up all the others. Quakers cannot be members of Parliament nor hold any office because it would mean taking an oath, and they will not swear. They are reduced to the necessity of earning money through commerce, and their children, made wealthy by their fathers' industry, want to enjoy things, have honours, buttons and cuffs; they are ashamed of being called Quakers and become Protestants to be in the fashion.

LETTER 5

*

ON THE ANGLICAN RELIGION

THIS is the land of sects. An Englishman, as a free man, goes to Heaven by whatever route he likes.

And yet, although every man here can serve God in his own way, their real religion, the one in which you get on in the world, is the Episcopal sect, called the Anglican Church or just 'the Church'. You cannot hold office in England or Ireland without being one of the Anglican faithful, and this, which is an excellent proof, has converted so many Nonconformists that today there is less than a twentieth of the nation outside the bosom of the dominant Church.

The Anglican clergy have retained many Catholic ceremonies, especially that of receiving tithes, with the most scrupulous attention. They have also the pious ambition to be the masters.

Moreover they foment to the best of their ability among their flock a holy zeal against Nonconformists. This zeal was considerable under the Tory government during the last years of Queen Anne, but it did not go beyond breaking the occasional window in heretical chapels, for sectarian fury finished in England with the civil wars, and under Queen Anne there remained only a few murmurs of a sea still choppy long after the storm has passed. When the Whigs and Tories split their country asunder, like the Guelphs and Ghibellines of old, religion inevitably came into the parties. The Tories were for the Episcopate, the Whigs wanted to abolish it, but when they became the masters they contented themselves with lowering its prestige.

At the time when Harley, Earl of Oxford,[9] and Lord Bolingbroke[10] drank to the health of the Tories, the Anglican Church looked upon them as the defenders of its holy privileges. The

37

assembly of lower clergy, which is a sort of priests' House of Commons, then had some influence; at least it enjoyed freedom to assemble, argue on controversial issues and from time to time to order a few impious books to be burnt, that is books written against itself. The present government, which is Whig, does not even allow these gentlemen to hold their assembly, and they are reduced, in the obscurity of their parishes, to the miserable job of praying to God for the government they would not at all mind overthrowing. As for the Bishops, twenty-six of them in all, they sit in the House of Lords despite the Whigs because the old abuse of regarding them as lords still persists, but they have no more power in the House than Dukes and Peers in the Parliament of Paris. There is one clause in the oath they swear to the State which tries the Christian patience of these gentlemen very much.

In this clause they promise to uphold the Church as established by law. There is hardly a single Bishop, Dean or Archdeacon who does not think he is that by divine right, and so it is a great mortification for them to be obliged to admit that they owe all to a miserable law made by profane laymen. A monk (Father Courayer) recently wrote a book intended to prove the validity and succession of Anglican ordinations. This book has been banned in France, but do you suppose it has pleased the government of England? Not at all. These wretched Whigs care very little whether the apostolic succession has been interrupted in their country or not, or whether Bishop Parker was consecrated in an alehouse (as some maintain) or in a church. They prefer Bishops to derive their authority from Parliament rather than from the Apostles. Lord B—— says that this idea of divine right would only serve to make tyrants in capes and rochets, but that the law makes citizens.

In morals the Anglican clergy are more virtuous than the French, and this is why: all the clergy are educated in the Universities of Oxford or Cambridge, far from the corruption of the capital. They are not called to the higher positions in the Church until very late in life and at an age when men have no other passion than avarice, when their ambition has little to feed on. Positions in this country are rewards for long service in the Church as well as the Army, and not many young men become bishops or colonels on leaving college. Moreover the clergy are almost all married; the uncouth manner they have acquired in the university and the lack of feminine society there mean that usually a bishop has to make do with his own wife. Priests do sometimes go to taverns because custom allows it, and if they get drunk it is solemnly and with no scandal.

That indefinable being, neither ecclesiastical nor secular, in a word what we call an Abbé, is an unknown species in England. Here clerical gentlemen are all decorous and almost all pedants. When they hear that in France young men notorious for their debauches and appointed to bishoprics through the intrigues of women, make love in public, find fun in composing tender love-songs, give long and exquisite suppers every night, and then go straight to pray for the light of the Holy Ghost and brazenly call themselves the successors of the Apostles, they thank God they are Protestants. But, of course, they are wicked heretics fit to be burned with all the devils, as Master François Rabelais says, and that is why I don't get mixed up in their affairs.

LETTER 6

*

ON THE PRESBYTERIANS

THE Anglican religion only extends to England and Ireland.
Presbyterianism is the dominant religion in Scotland. This
Presbyterianism is nothing more than pure Calvinism as it was
established in France and survives in Geneva. As the priests in
this sect receive very small stipends from their churches, and
so cannot live in the same luxury as bishops, they have taken
the natural course of decrying honours they cannot attain.
Picture the proud Diogenes trampling underfoot the pride of
Plato: the Scottish Presbyterians are not unlike that proud and
tattered reasoner. They treated Charles II with much less respect than Diogenes had treated Alexander. For when they took
up arms on his behalf against Cromwell who had deceived
them, they made the poor King put up with four sermons per
day, they forbade him to play cards, they sat him on the stool of
repentance, with the result that Charles soon grew tired of
being King of these pedants and escaped from their clutches
like a schoolboy playing truant.

Compared with a young and lusty French student bawling
in Theology Schools in the morning and singing with the ladies
at night, an English theologian is a Cato, but this Cato looks
like a gay young spark compared with a priest in Scotland. The
latter affects a solemn gait and scowling expression, wears a
huge hat, a long cloak over a short jacket, preaches through his
nose and gives the name of Whore of Babylon to all Churches
in which a few ecclesiastics are fortunate enough to have an
income of fifty thousand *livres* and in which the people are
good enough to put up with it and call them Monsignor, Your
Lordship, Your Eminence.

These gentry, who also have a few churches in England, have
brought solemn and austere airs into fashion in this country. It

is to them that we owe the sanctification of Sunday in the three kingdoms. On that day both work and play are forbidden, which is double the severity of Catholic Churches. There are no operas, plays or concerts in London on Sunday, even cards are so expressly forbidden that only people of standing and what are called respectable people, play on that day. The rest of the nation goes to the sermon, the tavern and the ladies of the town.

Although the Episcopal and Presbyterian sects are the two dominant ones in Great Britain, all the others are perfectly acceptable and live quite harmoniously together, whilst most of their preachers hate each other with almost as much cordiality as a Jansenist damns a Jesuit.

Go into the London Stock Exchange – a more respectable place than many a court – and you will see representatives from all nations gathered together for the utility of men. Here Jew, Mohammedan and Christian deal with each other as though they were all of the same faith, and only apply the word infidel to people who go bankrupt. Here the Presbyterian trusts the Anabaptist and the Anglican accepts a promise from the Quaker. On leaving these peaceful and free assemblies some go to the Synagogue and others for a drink, this one goes to be baptized in a great bath in the name of Father, Son and Holy Ghost, that one has his son's foreskin cut and has some Hebrew words he doesn't understand mumbled over the child, others go to their church and await the inspiration of God with their hats on, and everybody is happy.

If there were only one religion in England there would be danger of despotism, if there were two they would cut each other's throats, but there are thirty, and they live in peace and happiness.

LETTER 7

*

ON THE SOCINIANS, ARIANS OR ANTI-TRINITARIANS

THERE is a small sect here composed of priests and a few very clever laymen who do not adopt the name of Arians nor of Socinians, but are not at all of the opinion of St Athanasius in the matter of the Trinity, but tell you straight out that the Father is greater than the Son.

Do you remember a certain orthodox bishop who, to convince an Emperor about consubstantiation, took it into his head to chuck the Emperor's son under the chin and tweak his nose in the presence of His Sacred Majesty? The Emperor was on the point of being very angry with the bishop when the old boy uttered these fine, convincing words: 'My Lord, if your Majesty is angry because I am showing lack of respect for your son, how do you think God will treat those who refuse Jesus Christ the titles that are His due?' The people I am telling you about say that the holy bishop was very unwise, that his argument was anything but conclusive, and that the Emperor should have answered: 'Note that there are two ways of lacking respect for me, the first by not paying enough honour to my son, and the second by paying as much to him as to me.'

However that may be, the Arian faction is beginning to revive in England as well as in Holland and Poland. The great Mr Newton honoured this opinion by favouring it: this philosopher thought that the Unitarians reasoned more mathematically than we do. But the strongest upholder of the Arian doctrine is the illustrious Dr Clarke. This is a man of unswerving virtue and a gentle disposition, more interested in his opinions than excited about making converts, solely concerned with calculations and demonstrations – a real reasoning machine.

He is the author of a little understood but much admired book on the existence of God, and of another, better understood but rather looked down upon, about the truth of the Christian faith.

He has taken no part in fine scholastic controversies which our friend . . . calls hoary old nonsense, but has confined himself to publishing a book containing all the arguments in early times for and against the Unitarians, leaving to the reader the responsibility of counting the votes and deciding. This book of the Doctor's has gained him many supporters, but prevented him from becoming Archbishop of Canterbury. I think the Doctor has miscalculated and that it would have been better to be Primate of England than an Arian parish priest.

You see what revolutions take place in opinions as they do in Empires. The Arian faction, after three hundred years of triumph and twelve centuries of oblivion, is at last being reborn from its ashes, but it chooses a bad time to reappear in a period when everybody is sick and tired of sectarian disputes. This sect is still too small to have freedom of public assembly, but it will no doubt obtain it if it gets more numerous. However, just now people are so indifferent to all this that there is not much chance of success for a new religion or a revived one. Is it not amusing that Luther, Calvin, Zwingli, writers nobody can read, have founded sects that divide up Europe, that the ignorant Mahomet has given a religion to Asia and Africa, but that Newton, Clarke,[11] Locke, Leclerc, the greatest thinkers and finest writers of their age, have hardly managed to establish a little flock, and even that dwindles day by day?

That is what it means to come into the world at the right moment. If Cardinal de Retz reappeared today he would not collect together ten women in Paris.

If Cromwell, the man who had his King's head cut off and made himself sovereign, were born again, he would be an ordinary London merchant.

LETTER 8

*

ON PARLIAMENT

THE members of the English Parliament like to compare themselves, as far as they can, to the ancient Romans.

Not long ago Mr Shipping began his speech in the House of Commons with these words: 'The majesty of the English people would be hurt, etc.' The strangeness of the expression caused a loud burst of laughter but, by no means disconcerted, he repeated the same words in a firm tone, and there was no more laughing. I confess I see nothing in common between the majesty of the English people and that of the Romans, still less between their governments. There is a Senate in London, some members of which are suspected, no doubt wrongly, of selling their votes upon occasion as they did in Rome, but there the resemblance stops. Besides, the two nations seem to me entirely different, both in good and evil. The horrible madness of wars of religion was quite unknown to the Romans – that abomination was reserved for pious folk preaching humility and long suffering. Marius and Sulla, Pompey and Caesar, Antony and Augustus, did not fight to decide whether the *Flamen* should wear his shirt over his robe or his robe over his shirt, whether the sacred fowls should eat and drink or eat only before the auguries were taken. The English have in the past sent each other to be hanged at their Assizes and have destroyed each other in pitched battles over disputes of a similar kind. For a time the Episcopalian and Presbyterian sects distracted these serious-minded people. I fancy that such stupidity won't affect them any more; they seem to be getting wise at their own expense, and I cannot see them at all anxious to kill each other henceforth for the sake of syllogisms.

Here is a more essential difference between Rome and England which gives all the advantage to the latter: the outcome of civil wars in Rome was slavery, and that of the troubles in England liberty. The English nation is the only one on earth which has succeeded in controlling the power of kings by resisting them, which by effort after effort has at last established this wise system of government in which the prince, all-powerful for doing good, has his hands tied for doing evil, in which the aristocrats are great without arrogance and vassals, and in which the people share in the government without confusion.

The House of Lords and the Commons are the arbiters of the nation, the king is the super-arbiter. The Romans did not have this balance: the great and the plebs were always divided without any intermediate power to make them agree. The Roman Senate, which in its unjust and reprehensible pride refused to share anything with the plebeians, knew no other recipe for keeping them out of government than occupying them continually in foreign wars. They regarded the people as a wild beast they had to let loose on their neighbours for fear it might devour its masters. So the greatest fault of the government of the Romans made them into conquerors. It is because they were unfortunate at home that they became the masters of the world, until finally their disagreements turned them into slaves.

The government of England is not made for such great glory nor for such a terrible end; its object is not the brilliant folly of making conquests, but to prevent its neighbours from making any. These people are not only jealous of their own liberty but also of that of others. The English were fiercely hostile to Louis XIV simply because they thought he was ambitious. They made war against him with a light heart, certainly without self-interest.

No doubt liberty has only been established in England at a heavy cost, and the idol of despotic power has been drowned in seas of blood, but the English do not feel they have paid too high a price for good laws. The other nations have had no fewer troubles and have shed no less blood, but the blood they have poured out in the cause of their liberty has only cemented their servitude.

What becomes a revolution in England is only a sedition in

other countries. In Spain, in Barbary, in Turkey, a city takes up arms to defend its privileges; at once it is subjugated by mercenary soldiers, punished by executions, and the rest of the nation kisses its chains. The French think that the government of this island is stormier than the seas that surround it, and that is true. But that is so only when the King begins the storm, when he wants to become master of the vessel of which he is only the first pilot. The civil wars in France have been longer, more cruel, productive of greater crimes than those of England, but not one of these civil wars has had a moderate freedom as its object.

In the detestable times of Charles IX and Henri III the only question was whether one should be a slave of the Guises. As for the most recent conflict in Paris, it deserves nothing but jeers, and it looks to me like a lot of schoolboys rebelling against the headmaster and ending up with a whipping. Cardinal de Retz, with a great deal of misapplied cleverness and courage, a rebel for no reason, factious with no object, party leader without an army, intrigued for intrigue's sake and seemed to wage civil war for his own amusement. Parliament didn't know what he wanted, nor what he didn't want, he raised troops by decree and then disbanded them, he threatened and then begged forgiveness, he set a price on the head of Cardinal Mazarin and then complimented him with a ceremonial visit. Our civil wars under Charles VI had been cruel, those of the League were abominable, that of the Fronde was farcical.

What the French reproach the English for most of all is the execution of Charles I, who was treated by the victors as he would have treated them if he had won.

After all, consider on the one hand Charles I, defeated in a pitched battle, taken prisoner, tried and condemned at Westminster, and on the other the Emperor Henry VII, poisoned by his chaplain while receiving communion, Henri III, murdered by a monk who was the tool of a whole fanatical sect, thirty assassination plots against Henri IV, several of them put into action, and the last finally depriving France of that great king. Look at these crimes and judge for yourself.

LETTER 9

*

ON THE GOVERNMENT

THIS happy blend in the Government of England, this harmony between the Commons, the Lords and the King, was not always there. England lived in slavery for a long time; she has been the slave of the Romans, Saxons, Danes and French. William the Conqueror especially ruled over her with a rod of iron; he disposed of the wealth and the lives of his new subjects like an Oriental potentate; he forbade, on pain of death, any Englishman to dare to have a light or a fire in his dwelling after eight o'clock, either because he hoped by so doing to prevent their nocturnal assemblies, or because he wanted by means of such a curious prohibition to test how far the power of one man over other men can go.

It is true that before and since William the Conqueror the English have had Parliaments, and they boast about them as though these assemblies, called Parliaments and made up of ecclesiastical tyrants and robbers called barons, had been the guardians of public liberty and happiness.

The barbarians who swarmed down into the rest of Europe from the Baltic Sea brought with them these States or Parliaments about which there has been so much talk and which are so little understood. In those days kings were not despotic, it is true, but the people only groaned the more in a miserable thraldom. The chiefs of these savages who had ravaged France, Italy, Spain and England made themselves monarchs and their captains shared out amongst themselves the lands of the vanquished. Hence these margraves, lairds, barons, sub-tyrants who often fought against their king for the spoils of the nations. They were birds of prey fighting an eagle over sucking the blood of doves – each nation had a hundred tyrants instead of one master. The priests soon joined in the game. From earliest times the fate of the Gauls, Germans and islanders of England had been to be governed by their druids and by village chieftains, an early species of baron, but less tyrannical than their successors. These druids called themselves mediators between the Divinity and mankind, they made laws, they excommunicated, they condemned to death. The bishops gradually succeeded to their temporal authority in the Goth and Vandal governments. The Popes set themselves at their head, and with briefs, bulls and monks made kings tremble, deposed them, had them murdered and took for themselves as much money from Europe as they could. The imbecile Ine, one of the tyrants of the Heptarchy in England, was the first who on a pilgrimage to Rome agreed to pay Peter's pence (about an *écu* of our money) for each house in his territory. Soon the whole island followed his example. Little by little England became a papal province. The Holy Father sent his legates from time to time who raised exorbitant taxes. Finally John Lackland formally ceded his realm to His Holiness who had excommunicated him, but the barons, finding nothing in this for them, turned out that miserable king. They put in his place Louis VIII, father of Saint Louis, but they soon got tired of this newcomer and sent him back across the sea.

While the barons, bishops and popes were tearing England to pieces in this way, where they all wanted to dominate the people, the most numerous, most virtuous, even, and consequently most respectable part of mankind, made up of those who study laws and sciences, merchants, artisans, in a word all who were not tyrants, the people I mean, were regarded by them as animals lower than humanity. The Commons were then far from having any share in the government; they were serfs and their toil and blood belonged to their masters, who called themselves nobles. The majority of men in Europe were what they still are in many parts of the north, serfs of some lord, a kind of cattle bought and sold with the land. It took centuries to bring justice to mankind, to make people realize that it was horrible that the many should sow and the few reap. Is it not fortunate for the human race that the authority of these petty brigands was destroyed in France by the legitimate power of kings and people?

Happily, through the upheavals in which the quarrels of kings and grandees involved Empires, the fetters of the nations were more or less loosened – liberty was born in England out of the quarrels of the tyrants. The barons forced John Lackland and Henry III[12] to grant that famous Charter, the main object of which, it is true, was to make kings dependent upon the lords, but in which the rest of the nation were to some extent favoured in order that, should the occasion arise, they would take sides with their self-styled protectors. This great Charter, which is regarded as the sacred origin of English liberties, itself shows clearly how little liberty was understood. The title alone proves that the King thought he was absolute by right and that the barons and even the clergy only forced him to relinquish this so-called right because they were the stronger.

This is how Magna Carta begins: 'We grant of our own free will the following privileges to the Archbishops, Bishops, Abbots, Priors and Barons of our Realm, etc.'

In the articles of this Charter not a word is said about the House of Commons, which proves it did not yet exist or that it existed but with no power. Free men of England are mentioned, in itself a sorry demonstration that some existed who were not free. We see in Article 32 that these so-called free men owed services to their overlord. Such freedom still had much of slavery about it.

In Article 21 the King orders that his officers will henceforth only be able to take free men's horses and carts by force if they pay for them, and this ruling seemed a real liberty to people because it removed an even greater tyranny.

Henry VII, a fortunate usurper and skilful politician, who pretended to love the barons, but hated and feared them, bethought him to procure the transfer of their lands. In this way the villeins, who later acquired wealth by their toil, bought the residences of illustrious peers who had ruined themselves by their follies. Gradually all lands changed owners.

The House of Commons became more powerful day by day.

The families of the former peers died out in time, and as properly speaking only peers are nobles in England within the meaning of the law, there would be no nobility left in that country had not the Kings created new lords from time to time and preserved the peerage which they had formerly feared so much, so as to balance it against the Commons who had become too dangerous.

All these new peers, who form the Upper House, receive their title from the King but nothing else; hardly any of them possess the territory whose name they bear. One is Duke of Dorset and hasn't an inch of land in Dorset, another is Earl of some village and scarcely knows where this village is situated. They have power in Parliament and nowhere else.

You will hear nothing here about high, middle or low justice, or of the right to hunt over the land of a citizen who has no right to fire a shot in his own field.

A man is by no means exempt from paying certain taxes here simply because he is noble or because he is a priest. All taxes are fixed by the House of Commons which, though only second in rank, is first in prestige.

The Lords and Bishops may well reject the Bill from the Commons for taxation, but they may not change anything in it; they must either pass or reject it out of hand. When the Bill is confirmed by the Lords and approved by the King, then everybody pays. Everyone gives, not according to his rank (which is absurd) but according to his income. There is no arbitrary toll or capitation, but a real tax on landed property. This has all been assessed by the famous law of William III, and at below its market price.

The tax remains always the same, although income from land has risen, so nobody is downtrodden and nobody complains. The peasant's feet are not bruised by sabots, he eats white bread, he is well dressed, he is not reluctant to increase the number of his livestock or cover his roof with tiles for fear that his taxes will be raised the following year. There are country folk in this land worth about 200,000 francs, who are not too proud to continue tilling the soil that has enriched them and on which they live in freedom.

LETTER 10

*

ON COMMERCE

COMMERCE, which has enriched English citizens, has helped to make them free, and this freedom in its turn has extended commerce, and that has made the greatness of the nation. Commerce has gradually established the naval forces thanks to which the English are masters of the seas. At the present time they have nearly two hundred ships of the line. Posterity will perhaps learn with surprise that a small island which has no resources of its own except a little lead, some tin, some fuller's earth and coarse wool has through its commerce become powerful enough to send, in 1723, at one and the same time, three fleets to three extremities of the world, one before Gibraltar, conquered and held by its forces, another to Porto-Bello to cut off the treasures of the Indies from the King of Spain, and the third into the Baltic to prevent the Northern Powers from fighting.

When Louis XIV made Italy tremble and his armies, already masters of Savoy and Piedmont, were about to take Turin, Prince Eugene had to march from the middle of Germany to relieve the Duke of Savoy. He had no money, without which cities cannot be taken or defended, so he had recourse to English merchants. In just half an hour he was lent fifty million. With that he relieved Turin, beat the French and wrote this little note to those who had lent him this sum: 'Sirs, I have received your money and I flatter myself I have used it to your satisfaction.'

All this makes an English merchant justifiably proud and leads him to venture to compare himself, not without some reason, to a Roman citizen. And so the younger son of a Peer of the Realm does not look down on trade. Lord Townshend, Minister of State, has a brother who is happy to be a business man in the City. When Lord Oxford governed England, his younger brother was a factor at Aleppo, whence he refused to return and where he died.

This custom, which however is unfortunately beginning to disappear, seems monstrous to Germans who are mad about their quarterings; they cannot understand that the son of a Peer of England may only be a rich and influential bourgeois, whereas in Germany everybody is a Prince – one has seen as many as thirty Highnesses of the same name with nothing except coats of arms and pride.

In France anyone is a Marquis who wants to be, and whoever arrives in Paris with money to spend and a name ending in *-ac* or *-ille* can say: 'a man like me, a man of my standing', and loftily despise a business man, and the business man so often hears people speak disparagingly of his profession that he is foolish enough to blush. Yet I wonder which is the more useful to a nation, a well-powdered nobleman who knows exactly at what minute the King gets up and goes to bed, and who gives himself grand airs while playing the part of a slave in some Minister's antechamber, or a business man who enriches his country, issues orders from his office to Surat or Cairo, and contributes to the well-being of the world.

LETTER II

*

ON INOCULATION WITH SMALLPOX

It is whispered in Christian Europe that the English are mad and maniacs: mad because they give their children smallpox to prevent their getting it, and maniacs because they cheerfully communicate to their children a certain and terrible illness with the object of preventing an uncertain one. The English on their side say: 'The other Europeans are cowardly and unnatural: cowardly in that they are afraid of giving a little pain to their children, and unnatural because they expose them to death from smallpox some time in the future.' To judge who is right in this dispute, here is the history of this famous inoculation which is spoken of with such horror outside England.

From time immemorial the women of Circassia have been in the habit of giving smallpox to their children, even six months old, by making an incision in the arm and inserting into the incision a pustule that they have carefully removed from the body of another child. This pustule works in the arm where it is inserted like yeast in a piece of dough; it ferments and spreads its own qualities through the blood-stream. The spots of the child who has been given this artificial smallpox are used to carry the same disease to others. There is an almost continual circulation of it in Circassia, and when unfortunately there is no smallpox in the land people are as put out as they are elsewhere by a bad harvest.

What introduced a custom into Circassia which seems so strange to other nations is however a cause common to the whole world: mother-love and self-interest.

The Circassians are poor and their daughters are beautiful, and so they use them as their chief export. They supply beauties to the harems of the Grand Turk, the Sophy of Persia and those who are rich enough to buy and keep this precious merchandise.

With the most honourable intentions they train these girls to perform dances full of lasciviousness and sensuousness, to rekindle by all the most voluptuous artifices the desires of the high and mighty masters for whom they are destined. These poor creatures go over their lesson with their mother every day, just as our little girls repeat their catechism, not understanding a word of it.

Now it often happened that a father and mother, having taken a great deal of trouble to give their children a good upbringing, suddenly saw their hopes frustrated. Smallpox came into the family, one daughter died of it, another lost an eye, a third recovered but with a swollen nose, and the poor folk were ruined, with no resources. Often it even happened, when smallpox became epidemic, that trade was interrupted for several years, which caused a notable depletion in the seraglios of Persia and Turkey.

A commercial nation is always very alive to its interests and neglects none of the knowledge that can be useful in its business. The Circassians noticed that out of a thousand persons, hardly a single one was attacked twice by serious smallpox, that certainly people can develop three or four slight attacks, but never two serious and dangerous ones, in a word that the true disease never occurs twice in a lifetime. Furthermore, they noticed that when smallpox attacks are very mild and the outbreak finds only a delicate and thin skin to pierce, it leaves no mark upon the face. From these natural observations they concluded that if a child of six months or a year had a mild attack it would not die and would not be marked, and would be immune from the disease for the rest of its days.

To preserve the life and beauty of their children it only remained, then, to give them smallpox at an early age, and that is what they did by inserting into the child's body a pustule taken from the most perfect and at the same time most favourable case of smallpox that could be found. The experiment was bound to succeed. The Turks, who are sensible people, soon adopted this custom, and today there is not a Pasha in Constantinople who does not give smallpox to his son and daughter as soon as they are weaned.

Some people maintain that the Circassians originally took this custom from the Arabs, but we leave this historical point to be cleared up by some learned Benedictine, who will doubtless compose several folio volumes on the subject, with proofs. All I have to say on this matter is that at the beginning of the reign of George I, Lady Wortley Montagu,[13] one of the most intelligent women in England, and with a powerful intellect into the bargain, then living with her husband at the Embassy in Constantinople, decided without any hesitation to give smallpox to a child she had given birth to in that country. In vain did her chaplain point out that this procedure was not Christian and so could only succeed on infidels; Lady Wortley Montagu's son thrived on it. Back in London this lady mentioned her experiment to the Princess of Wales, who is now Queen. It must be admitted that, titles and crowns apart, this Princess was born to encourage all the arts and do good to mankind. She is a delightful philosopher on the throne. She has never lost a chance of learning or of exercising her generosity. It was she who, hearing that a daughter of Milton was still alive and living in poverty, at once sent her a handsome present, she who is the patron of poor Father Courayer, she who deigned to mediate between Dr Clarke and Leibnitz. As soon as she heard about inoculation or insertion of smallpox, she tried it out on four criminals condemned to death. She saved their lives twice over, for not only did she snatch them from the gibbet but thanks to this artificial smallpox she prevented the natural death from it that they would probably have suffered later in their lives.

Once assured of the practical success of this test, the Princess had her own children inoculated: England followed her example, and since then at least ten thousand children of good family thus owe their lives to the Queen and Lady Wortley Montagu, and as many girls are indebted to them for their beauty.

Out of a hundred people in the world at least sixty have

smallpox, and of these sixty, twenty die of it in the flower of their youth and twenty keep the unpleasant marks for ever. That makes one fifth of all human beings that this disease kills or permanently disfigures. Of all those inoculated in Turkey or England not one dies unless he is infirm and predisposed to die anyway, nobody is disfigured, nobody has smallpox a second time, assuming that the inoculation was properly done. So it is certain that if some French Ambassador's wife had brought back this secret from Constantinople to Paris, she would have done the nation a lasting service. The Duc de Villequier, father of the present Duc d'Aumont and one of the most balanced and healthiest men in France, would not have died in the prime of life.

The Prince de Soubise, who enjoyed the most perfect health, would not have been carried off at twenty-five; Monseigneur, grandfather of Louis XV, would not have been buried in his fiftieth year; twenty thousand people who died in Paris in 1723 would still be alive. What! Aren't the French fond of life? Do their women not care about their beauty? Indeed we are strange folk! Perhaps in ten years' time we shall adopt this English method if the priests and doctors permit, or else in three months' time the French will use inoculation because they fancy it, if the English get tired of it through fickleness.

I understand that the Chinese have had this custom for a hundred years. The example of a nation that passes for the wisest and most strictly governed in the universe is a great thing in its favour. It is true that the Chinese set about it in a different way; they don't make an incision but make the subject take in smallpox through the nose, like snuff. This is a more pleasant way, but it comes to the same thing and serves just as well to confirm that if inoculation had been practised in France the lives of thousands of people would have been saved.

LETTER 12

*

ON CHANCELLOR BACON

Not long ago, in a distinguished company, they were discussing this time-honoured and frivolous question: who was the greatest man, Caesar, Alexander, Tamburlaine, Cromwell, etc.

Somebody answered that it was unquestionably Isaac Newton. He was right, for if true greatness consists in having received from heaven a powerful genius and in having used it to enlighten himself and others, a man such as Newton, the like of whom is scarcely to be found in ten centuries, is the truly great man, and these politicians and conquerors, in which no period has been lacking, are usually nothing more than illustrious criminals. It is to the man who rules over minds by the power of truth, not to those who enslave men by violence, it is to the man who understands the universe and not to those who disfigure it, that we owe our respect.

Since you ask me to tell you about the famous men England has given birth to, I shall begin with men like Bacon, Locke, Newton, etc. The generals and ministers will come in their turn.

I must begin with the famous Earl of Verulam, known in Europe by the name of Bacon, his family name. He was the son of the Lord Keeper of the Great Seal, and for a long time was Chancellor under King James I. Yet, amid the intrigues of Court and the preoccupations of his office, enough to absorb a man completely, he found time to be a great scientific thinker, a good historian and an elegant writer, and what is even more astonishing, he lived in an age when the art of good writing was hardly known, still less scientific thought. As is customary among men, he has been more respected since his death than in his lifetime. His enemies were at Court in London, his admirers in the whole of Europe.

When the Marquis d'Effiat conducted to England Princess Marie, daughter of Henry the Great, who was to marry the Prince of Wales, this minister went and paid a visit to Bacon who, being ill in bed, received him with the curtains drawn. 'You are like the angels,' said d'Effiat, 'one always hears about them, they are thought to be much superior to men, but one never has the consolation of seeing them.'

You know, Monsieur, how Bacon was accused of a crime ill befitting a philosopher, that of letting himself be corrupted by money, you know how he was condemned by the House of Lords to a fine of about 400,000 *livres* of our money, and to lose his rank as Chancellor and Peer.

Today the English so revere his memory that they are unwilling to admit that he may have been guilty. If you ask me what I think about it I will answer by borrowing a word I heard Lord Bolingbroke say. In his presence the conversation touched on the avarice of which the Duke of Marlborough was accused, and they gave examples of it and asked Lord Bolingbroke to bear witness because, having been his declared enemy, he could perhaps express an opinion without impropriety. 'He was such a great man,' was the answer, 'that I have forgotten his vices.'

So I will confine myself to telling you what earned for Chancellor Bacon the respect of Europe.

The best and most remarkable of his works is the one which is the least read today and the least useful: I refer to his *Novum Scientiarum Organum*. It is the scaffolding by means of which modern scientific thought has been built, and when that edifice had been raised, at least in part, the scaffolding ceased to be of any use.

Chancellor Bacon did not yet understand nature, but he knew and pointed out the roads leading to it. He had very early scorned what the Universities called Philosophy, and he did everything in his power to prevent these institutions, set up for the perfection of human reason, from continuing to spoil it with their *quiddities*, their *abhorrence of a vacuum*, their *substantial forms* and all the inappropriate expressions which not only ignorance made respectable, but which a ridiculous confusion with religion had made almost sacred.

He is the father of experimental philosophy. It is true that some amazing secrets had been discovered before his time. Men had invented the compass, printing, engraving, oil-painting, mirrors, the art of restoring to some extent sight to the aged by glasses, called spectacles, gunpowder, etc. Men had searched for, found and conquered a new world. Who would not have thought that these sublime discoveries had been made by the greatest scientists in times much more enlightened than ours? Not at all; it was in the age of the most mindless barbarism that these great changes were made on the earth. Chance alone produced almost all these inventions, and there is even every appearance that what may be called chance played a large part in the discovery of America – at all events it has always been believed that Christopher Columbus only undertook his voyage on the word of a captain who had been cast ashore by a storm on the Caribbean islands.

However that may be, men already knew how to get to the ends of the earth, how to destroy cities with an artificial thunder more terrible than the real thing, but they knew nothing about the circulation of the blood, the weight of the atmosphere, the laws of dynamics, the number of the planets, etc., and a man who upheld a thesis on the categories of Aristotle, on the universal *a parte rei* or some other such idiocy, was regarded as a prodigy.

The most wonderful and useful inventions are not those which do most honour to the human mind.

It is to a mechanical instinct, which exists in most men, that we owe all the skills, and not to a sound philosophy.

The discovery of fire, the art of making bread, of melting and forging metals, building houses, the invention of the shuttle, are of much more practical necessity than printing or the compass, yet these skills were invented by men still in a state of savagery.

Since then what prodigious use the Greeks and Romans have made of mechanical inventions! Yet they thought in their time that the skies were of crystal and the stars were little lamps which sometimes fell down into the sea, and one of their great philosophers, after much research, had discovered that the heavenly bodies were pebbles that had come loose from the earth.

In a word, nobody before Chancellor Bacon had grasped experimental science, and of all the practical applications made since, scarcely one is not foreshadowed in his book. He had made several himself; he made a kind of pneumatic machine by means of which he guessed at the elasticity of the air, and he circled all round the discovery of its weight, indeed he almost had it, but the truth was seized upon by Torricelli. Not long afterwards experimental physics was suddenly taken up simultaneously in almost all parts of Europe. It was a hidden treasure the existence of which Bacon had suspected and which all the scientists, encouraged by his promise, strove to dig out.

But what has surprised me most has been to see in his book, in explicit terms, this new law of attraction for the invention of which Newton has the credit.

'We must try to discover,' says Bacon, 'whether there might not be a kind of magnetic force operating between the earth and things with weight, between the moon and the ocean, between the planets, etc.'

Elsewhere he says:

It must either be that heavy bodies are impelled towards the centre of the earth, or that they are mutually attracted by it, and in the latter case it is evident that the nearer these falling bodies get to the earth the more strongly they are attracted to each other. We must see whether the same clock with weights will go faster at the top of a mountain or at the bottom of a mine; it is probable, if the pull of the weights decreases on the mountain and increases in the mine, that the earth has a real attraction.

This precursor of science was also an elegant writer, a historian and a wit.

His *Essays* are very well thought of, but they are intended to instruct rather than to please, and being neither a satire on human nature like the *Maxims* of La Rochefoucauld, nor a school for sceptics like Montaigne, they are less often read than those two ingenious books.

His *History of Henry VII* passed for a masterpiece, but I should be much mistaken if it could be compared with the work of our illustrious de Thou.[14]

Speaking of the famous impostor Parkins,[15] a Jew by birth, who so brazenly assumed the title of Richard IV, King of England, encouraged by the Duchess of Burgundy, and who laid claim to the crown of Henry VII, this is how Chancellor Bacon expresses himself:

At about this time, King Henry was haunted by evil spirits through the magic of the Duchess of Burgundy, who conjured up from the underworld the shade of Edward IV to torment King Henry. When the Duchess of Burgundy had instructed Parkins she began to deliberate about which region of the sky she would make the comet come from, and she resolved that it would burst forth first on the horizon of Ireland.

It seems to me that our wise de Thou does not go in for all this rigmarole that was formerly taken as inspired, but is nowadays rightly called mumbo-jumbo.

LETTER 13

*

ON MR LOCKE

NEVER, perhaps, has a wiser, more methodical mind, a more precise logician existed than Mr Locke, yet he was not a great mathematician. He had never been able to put up with the tedium of calculations or the sterility of mathematical truths which do not at first offer anything appreciable to the mind, and nobody has proved better than he that one can possess the geometrical mind without the help of geometry. Before him great philosophers had decided exactly what the human soul is, but since they knew nothing whatever about it it is only to be expected that they all had different views.

In Greece, cradle of arts and errors, and where they carried to such lengths the greatness and the stupidity of the human mind, they reasoned about the soul as we do.

The divine Anaxagoras, to whom an altar was erected because he had taught men that the sun was larger than the Peloponnese, that snow was black and the skies made of stone, affirmed that the soul was an aerial spirit yet immortal.

Diogenes, a different one from the one who turned Cynic after being a coiner, averred that the soul was a portion of the very stuff of God. That idea at least was brilliant.

Epicurus made it up from particles, like the body. Aristotle, who has been explained in a thousand different ways because he was unintelligible, believed, if we consult some of his disciples, that the understanding of all men was one and the same substance.

The divine Plato, master of the divine Aristotle, and the divine Socrates, master of the divine Plato, said that the soul was corporal and eternal – Socrates' daemon had no doubt told him how things were. There are people, it is true, who maintain that a man who boasted about his familiar spirit was undoubtedly a madman or a rogue, but those people are over-particular.

As for our Fathers of the Church, several of them in the earliest times believed the human soul, the Angels and God were corporal.

The world grows steadily more refined. St Bernard, according to Père Mabillon,[16] taught about the soul that after death it did not see God in Heaven but only conversed with the humanity of Jesus Christ; this time his word was not taken for it, for the adventure of the Crusades had somewhat discredited his oracles. A thousand Scholastics came after him, like the Irrefragable Doctor, the Subtle Doctor, the Angelic Doctor, the Seraphic Doctor, the Cherubic Doctor, who were all quite sure they knew the soul very clearly, but who took care to talk about it as though they did not wish anybody to understand anything of it.

Our Descartes, born to uncover the errors of antiquity but to substitute his own, and spurred on by that systematizing mind which blinds the greatest of men, imagined he had demonstrated that the soul was the same thing as thought, just as matter, for him, is the same thing as space. He affirmed that we think all the time, and that the soul comes into the body already endowed with all the metaphysical notions, knowing God, space, the infinite, having all the abstract ideas, full, in fact, of learning which unfortunately it forgets on leaving its mother's womb.

M. Malebranche, of the Oratory, in his sublime illusions, not only admitted the existence of innate ideas but had no doubt that we saw everything in God and that God, so to speak, was our soul.

So many thinkers having written the novel of the soul, a wise man has appeared who has modestly written its history. Locke has expounded human understanding to mankind as an excellent anatomist explains the mechanism of the human body. At all points he calls in the light of physics, he sometimes ventures to speak affirmatively, but he also dares to doubt. Instead of defining at one fell swoop what we don't know, he examines by degrees what we want to know. He takes a child at the moment of birth and follows step by step the progress of its understanding, he sees what the child has in common with the animals and in what it is superior to them, he consults especially his own experience, the consciousness of his own thought.

'I let those who know more about it than I do,' he says, 'argue whether our souls exist before or after the organization of our bodies, but I confess that I have been endowed with one of those coarse souls that are not thinking all the time, and am even unfortunate enough not to think it any more necessary for the soul to be always thinking than it is for the body to be always in motion.'

For myself I am proud of the honour of being as stupid as Locke in this matter. Nobody will persuade me that I am always thinking, and I feel no more disposed than he to imagine that a few weeks after my conception I was a most sapient soul, already knowing a thousand things that I forgot at birth, having quite pointlessly possessed in the uterus knowledge that escaped me as soon as I was in a position to need it and which I have never been able to regain properly since.

Locke, having destroyed innate ideas, having abandoned the vanity of believing that we are always thinking, establishes that all our ideas come to us via the senses, examines our simple ideas and those that are complex, follows the human mind in all its operations, shows how imperfect are the languages men speak and how we misuse terms at every moment.

Finally he considers the extent, or rather the non-existence, of human knowledge. It is in this chapter that he modestly ventures these words: *We shall probably never be able to know whether a purely material being thinks or not.*

This wise remark seemed to more than one theologian a scandalous declaration that the soul is material and mortal.

Some Englishmen, devout after their own fashion, sounded the alarm. The superstitious in society are what cowards are in an army: they feel and pass on panic terrors. There was an outcry that Locke sought to overthrow religion. But religion had nothing to do with this affair; it was a purely philosophical question quite independent of faith and revelation, simply a matter of examining without rancour whether there is any contradiction in saying: *matter can think*, and whether God can communicate thought to matter. But theologians too often begin by saying that God is outraged when you don't share their point of view. This is all too much like those poetasters who screamed that because he laughed at them Despréaux[17] insulted the King.

Dr Stillingfleet[18] earned the reputation of being a moderate theologian because he had not positively insulted Locke. He entered the lists against him but was beaten, for he reasoned as a Doctor of Divinity and Locke did so as a philosopher who was well acquainted with the strength and weakness of the human mind and fought with weapons of which he knew the quality.

If I dared to speak after Mr Locke on such a delicate subject I would say: men have argued for a long time about the nature and immortality of the soul. As to its immortality, this is impossible to demonstrate since its nature is still in dispute, and surely we must know a created being thoroughly in order to decide whether it is immortal or not. Human reason is so incapable of demonstrating unaided the immortality of the soul that religion has been obliged to reveal it to us. The common good of all men requires belief in the immortal soul; faith orders it, nothing more is needed, the thing is decided. But the same is not the case with its nature; it matters little to religion what substance the soul is made of provided it be virtuous. It is a clock that has been given us to keep right, but the maker has not told us what the spring of this clock is made of.

I am a body and I think. I know no more than that. Shall I then attribute to an unknown cause what I can so easily attribute to the one secondary cause I know? Here all the philosophers of the School interrupt me by arguing thus: 'In the body there is nothing but volume and solidity, and that can only have motion and shape. Now motion and shape, volume and solidity cannot produce a thought, therefore the soul cannot be matter.' All this grand argument repeated so many times simply amounts to this: 'I don't understand matter at all, I imperfectly guess at some of its properties. Now, I don't know at all whether these properties can be connected with thought, therefore because I know nothing about it I affirm positively that matter cannot think.' That is a clear statement of the School's way of thinking. Locke would simply say to these gentlemen: 'Admit at any rate that you are as ignorant as I am; neither your imagination nor mine can conceive how a body has ideas, and do you understand any the more how a substance, whatever it be, has ideas? You don't comprehend either matter or spirit, how then can you dare to affirm anything whatever?'

The superstitious come in their turn and say that those who suspect that one can think with the body alone should be burnt for the good of their souls. But what would they say if it were themselves who were guilty of irreligion? And indeed what kind of man will dare to affirm, without absurd impiety, that it is impossible for the Creator to endow matter with thought and feeling? Consider, I beg of you, you people who put such a limit on the power of the Creator, what a pass you bring yourselves to! The animals have the same organs as ourselves, the same feelings, the same perceptions; they have memory, they put together a few ideas. If God has been unable to animate matter and give it feeling, you are left with one of two things: either the animals are pure machines or they have a spiritual soul.

It seems almost proven to me that the animals cannot be simple machines. Here is my proof: God has provided them with exactly the same organs of feeling as ours. So if they cannot feel, God has done a pointless job. Now by your own admission God does nothing in vain. Therefore He has not made all these organs of feeling so that there should be no feelings. Therefore the animals are not simple machines.

The animals, according to you, cannot have a spiritual soul; so, in spite of you, there remains nothing else to say except that God has given to the organs of animals, who are matter, the faculty of feeling and perceiving, which in them you call instinct.

Well then, what can prevent God from communicating to our more delicate organs this faculty of feeling, perceiving and thinking that we call human reason? Whichever way you turn you are obliged to admit your own ignorance and the immense power of the Creator. So cease revolting against the wise and moderate philosophy of Locke; far from being hostile to religion it would act as a proof if religion needed one, for what philosophy is more religious than one which, affirming only what it can clearly conceive, and freely confessing its own weakness, tells you that you must come back to God as soon as you examine first principles?

Moreover it must never be feared that any philosophical sentiment can harm the religion of a country. Our mysteries may well clash with our demonstrations, but they are no less revered by Christian philosophers, who know that the aims of reason and faith are different by nature. Philosophers will never form a religious sect. Why? Because they do not write for the people and are devoid of emotional fire.

Divide mankind into twenty parts: nineteen consist of men who work with their hands and will never know that there is a Locke in the world, and in the remaining twentieth part how few men will you find who are readers! And of those who read, twenty read novels to one who studies philosophy. The number of those who think is exceedingly small, and they are not interested in upsetting the world.

It is not Montaigne, nor Locke, nor Bayle, nor Spinoza, nor Hobbes, nor Lord Shaftesbury, nor Mr Collins, nor Mr Toland,[19] etc, who have carried the torch of discord into their countries; it is in the main the theologians who, having begun by aiming at being heads of a sect, soon aimed at being heads of a party. Indeed, all the books of the modern philosophers put together will never make as much noise in the world as a simple dispute made some time ago among the Franciscans about the cut of their sleeves and cowls.

LETTER 14

*

ON DESCARTES AND NEWTON

A Frenchman arriving in London finds things very different, in natural science as in everything else. He has left the world full, he finds it empty. In Paris they see the universe as composed of vortices of subtle matter, in London they see nothing of the kind. For us it is the pressure of the moon that causes the tides of the sea; for the English it is the sea that gravitates towards the moon, so that when you think that the moon should give us a high tide, these gentlemen think you should have a low one. Unfortunately this cannot be verified, for to check this it would have been necessary to examine the moon and the tides at the first moment of creation.

Furthermore, you will note that the sun, which in France doesn't come into the picture at all, here plays its fair share. For your Cartesians everything is moved by an impulsion you don't really understand, for Mr Newton it is by gravitation, the cause of which is hardly better known. In Paris you see the earth shaped like a melon, in London it is flattened on two sides. For a Cartesian light exists in the air, for a Newtonian it comes from the sun in six and a half minutes. Your chemistry performs all its operations with acids, alkalis and subtle matter; gravitation dominates even English chemistry.

The very essence of things has totally changed. You fail to agree both on the definition of the soul and on that of matter. Descartes affirms that the soul is the same thing as thought, and Locke proves to him fairly satisfactorily the opposite.

Descartes also affirms that volume alone makes matter, Newton adds solidity. There you have some appalling clashes.

Non nostrum inter vos tantas componere lites.

This Newton, destroyer of the Cartesian system, died in

March last year, 1727. He lived honoured by his compatriots and was buried like a king who had done well by his subjects.

People here have eagerly read and translated into English the *Eulogy of Newton* that M. de Fontenelle delivered in the Académie des Sciences.[20] In England it was expected that the verdict of M. de Fontenelle would be a solemn declaration of the superiority of English natural science. But when it was realized that he compared Descartes with Newton the whole Royal Society in London rose up in arms. Far from agreeing with this judgement they criticized the discourse. Several even (not the most scientific) were shocked by the comparison simply because Descartes was a Frenchman.

It must be admitted that these two great men were very different in their behaviour, their fortune and their philosophy.

Descartes was born with a lively, strong imagination, which made him a remarkable man in his private life as well as in his manner of reasoning. This imagination could not be concealed even in his philosophical writings, where ingenious and brilliant illustrations occur at every moment. Nature had made him almost a poet, and indeed he composed for the Queen of Sweden an entertainment in verse which for the honour of his memory has not been printed.

For a time he tried the career of arms, and having later become the complete philosopher he did not think it unworthy of him to make love. His mistress gave him a daughter named Francine, who died young and whose loss grieved him deeply. Thus he experienced everything pertaining to mankind.

For a long time he believed it necessary to avoid the company of men, and especially his own country, so as to meditate in freedom. He was right; the men of his time did not know enough to enlighten him, and could scarcely do anything but harm him.

He left France because he sought the truth, which was being persecuted there by the wretched philosophy of the School, but he found no more reason in the universities of Holland, to which he retreated. For at the time when in France they condemned the only propositions in his philosophy that were true, he was also persecuted by the self-styled philosophers of Holland, who understood him no better and who, seeing his glory nearer at hand, hated his person the more. He was obliged to leave Utrecht. He was accused of atheism, and this man who had devoted all the penetration of his mind to seeking new proofs of the existence of a God, was suspected of not recognizing any.

So much persecution suggested very great merit and a brilliant reputation, and he had both. Reason did pierce a little into the world through the darkness of the School and the prejudices of popular superstition. At length his name became so well known that they tried to lure him back to France by bribes. He was offered a pension of 1000 *écus*, he came on that understanding, paid the fee for a patent which was for sale at that time, did not receive the pension and returned to work in his solitude in North Holland at the time when the great Galileo, aged eighty, was languishing in the prisons of the Inquisition for having demonstrated the movement of the earth. Finally he died in Stockholm – a premature death caused by faulty diet – amid a few hostile scientists and tended by a doctor who hated him.

The career of Sir Isaac Newton was quite different. He lived to be eighty-five, always tranquil, happy and honoured in his own country.

His great good fortune was not only to be born in a free country, but at a time when, scholastic extravagances being banished, reason alone was cultivated and society could only be his pupil and not his enemy.

A remarkable contrast between him and Descartes is that in the course of such a long life he had neither passion nor weakness; he never went near any woman. I have heard that confirmed by the doctor and the surgeon who were with him when he died. One can admire Newton for that, but must not blame Descartes.

In England, public opinion of the two of them is that the first was a dreamer and the other a sage.

Very few people in London read Descartes, whose works, practically speaking, have become out of date. Very few read Newton either, because much knowledge is necessary to understand him. However, everybody talks about them, conceding nothing to the Frenchman and everything to the Englishman. There are people who think that if we are no longer content with the abhorrence of a vacuum, if we know that the air has weight, if we use a telescope, it is all due to Newton. Here he is the Hercules of the fable, to whom the ignorant attributed all the deeds of the other heroes.

In a criticism made in London of the discourse of M. de Fontenelle, people have dared to assert that Descartes was not a great mathematician. People who talk like that can be reproached for beating their own nurse. Descartes covered as much ground from the point where he found mathematics to where he took it as Newton after him. He is the first to have found the way of expressing curves by algebraical equations. His mathematics, now common knowledge thanks to him, was in his time so profound that no professor dared undertake to explain it, and only Schooten in Holland and Fermat in France understood it.

He carried this spirit of mathematics and invention into dioptrics, which became in his hands quite a new art, and if he committed some errors it is because a man who discovers new territories cannot suddenly grasp every detail of them: those who come after him and make these lands fertile do at least owe their discovery to him. I will not deny that all the other works of Descartes are full of errors.

Mathematics was a guide that he himself had to some extent formed, and which would certainly have led him in his physical researches, but he finally abandoned this guide and gave himself up to a fixed system. Thereafter his philosophy was nothing more than an ingenious novel, at the best only plausible to ignoramuses. He was wrong about the nature of the soul, proofs of the existence of God, matter, the laws of dynamics, the nature of light; he accepted innate ideas, invented new elements, created a world and made man to his own specification, and it is said, rightly, that Descartes' man is only Descartes' man and far removed from true man.

He carried his metaphysical errors to the point of maintaining that two and two only make four because God has willed it so. But it is not too much to say that he was admirable even in his errors. He was wrong, but at least methodically and with a logical mind; he destroyed the absurd fancies with which youth had been beguiled for two thousand years, he taught the men of his time to reason and to use his own weapons against himself. He did not pay in good money, but it is no small thing to have denounced the counterfeit.

I don't think we really dare compare in any way his philosophy with that of Newton: the first is a sketch, the second is a masterpiece. But the man who set us on the road to the truth is perhaps as noteworthy as the one who since then has been to the end of the road.

Descartes gave sight to the blind; they saw the shortcomings of antiquity and his own. The path he opened has since become measureless. The little book by Rohaut was for a time a complete manual of physics; today all the collected writings of the Academies of Europe put together don't even make a beginning of a system. As one has gone deeper into this abyss it has revealed its infinity. We are about to see what Newton has quarried out of this chasm.

ON THE SYSTEM OF GRAVITATION

THE discoveries of Sir Isaac Newton, which have earned him such a universal reputation, concern the system of the world, light, infinity in mathematics and finally chronology, with which he toyed for relaxation.

I am going to tell you (if I can without verbiage) the little I have been able to gather about all these sublime ideas.

Concerning the system of our world, arguments had been going on for a long time on the basic cause which makes all the planets turn and keeps them in their orbits, and on that which in our own world makes all bodies fall on to the surface of the earth.

The system of Descartes, interpreted and very much modified since his time, seemed to offer a plausible reason for these phenomena, and this reason seemed all the truer for being simple and intelligible to all. But in natural philosophy one should mistrust what one feels and understands too easily, just as much as the things one does not understand.

Weight, the acceleration of bodies falling to the ground, the revolution of the planets in their orbits, their rotation upon their axes, these things are merely movement. Now, movement is inconceivable without impulsion, therefore all these bodies are propelled. But by what? All space is filled, so it is full of very subtle matter, since we do not perceive it. So this matter moves from west to east, since all the planets are moved from west to east. So, from supposition to supposition and probability, the imagination has produced a vast vortex of subtle matter in which the planets are borne along round the sun. In addition another small vortex has been created which swims in the larger one and revolves daily round the planet. When all that is said and done, it is affirmed that weight depends upon this daily movement, for, it is said, the subtle matter that turns round our little vortex must travel seventeen times faster than the earth. Now if it goes seventeen times faster than the earth it must have an incomparably greater centrifugal force and consequently propel all bodies towards the earth. That is the cause of weight in the Cartesian system.

But before calculating the centrifugal force and the velocity of this subtle matter one ought to have made sure it existed, and, assuming it exists, it is still demonstrably false that it can be the cause of weight.

Newton appears to have demolished for good all these vortices, large and small, the one which bears each planet round the sun as well as the one which makes each planet turn on its own axis.

Firstly, concerning the supposed lesser vortex round the earth, it is proved that it must gradually lose its impetus, it is proved that if the earth floats in a fluid, this fluid must be of the same density as the earth, and if this fluid is of the same density, all the bodies that we move must encounter extreme resistance, that is to say that we should need a lever as long as the earth to lift a pound weight.

Secondly, concerning the greater vortices, they are even more fanciful. It is impossible to reconcile them with Kepler's laws, the truth of which is patent. Newton shows that the revolution of the fluid in which Jupiter is supposed to be carried is not the same in relation to that of the earth as the revolution of Jupiter itself is to that of the earth.

He proves that as all the planets perform their revolutions in ellipses and are consequently much further from each other in their *aphelia* and much nearer in their *perihelia*, the earth, for example, should travel faster when it is nearer Venus and Mars, since the fluid carrying it, being under more pressure, must move faster. Yet it is just at that time that the motion of the earth is at its slowest.

He proves that there is no celestial matter going from the west to the east, as the comets cross these spaces sometimes from east to west and sometimes from north to south.

Finally, the better to settle if possible every difficulty, he proves, or at least makes it highly probable, even by experiments, that a plenum cannot possibly exist, and he brings back the vacuum, which Aristotle and Descartes had banished from the universe.

Having for all these reasons and many others demolished the vortices of Cartesianism, he despaired of ever being able to know whether there is a secret principle in nature which at one and the same time causes the motion of all the heavenly bodies and weight on the earth. Having retired to the country near Cambridge in 1666, he was walking in his garden, saw some fruit falling from a tree and let himself drift into a profound meditation on this weight, the cause of which all the scientists have vainly sought for so long and about which ordinary people never even suspect there is any mystery. He said to himself: 'From whatever height in our hemisphere these bodies might fall, their fall would certainly be in the progression discovered by Galileo, and the spaces traversed by them would be equal to the square of the time taken. This force which makes heavy bodies descend is the same, with no appreciable diminution, at whatever depth one may be in the earth and on the highest mountain. Why shouldn't this force stretch right up to the moon? And if it is true that it reaches as far as that, is it not highly probable that this force keeps the moon in its orbit and determines its movement? But if the moon obeys this principle, whatever it may be, is it not also very reasonable to think that the other planets are similarly influenced?

'If this force exists it must (as is proved, moreover) increase in inverse ratio to the squares of the distances. So it only remains to examine the distance covered by a heavy body falling to the ground from a medium height, and that covered in the same time by a body falling from the orbit of the moon. To know this it only remains to have the measurements of the earth and the distance from the moon to the earth.'

That is how Newton reasoned. But in England at that time there existed only very erroneous measurements of our globe. People relied on the faulty reckoning of pilots, who counted sixty English miles to a degree, whereas they should have counted nearly seventy. As this false calculation did not agree with the conclusions Newton wanted to draw, he abandoned them. A mediocre scientist, motivated solely by vanity, would have made the measurements of the earth fit in with his system as best he could. Newton preferred to abandon his project for the time being. But since M. Picard[21] had measured the earth accurately by tracing this meridian, which is such an honour for France, Newton took up his first ideas again and found what he wanted with the calculations of M. Picard. This is a thing that still seems admirable to me; to have discovered such sublime truths with a quadrant and a bit of arithmetic.

The circumference of the earth is 123,249,600 Paris feet. From that alone the whole system of gravitation can follow.

The circumference of the earth is known, that of the orbit of the moon is known and the diameter of this orbit. One revolution of the moon in this orbit takes twenty-seven days, seven hours, forty-three minutes. So it is clear that the moon in its mean path travels at 197,960 Paris feet per minute and by a known theorem it is clear that the central force that would make a body fall from the height of the moon would make it fall only fifteen Paris feet in the first minute.

Now if the law by which bodies weigh, gravitate, attract each other in inverse ratio to the squares of the distances is true, if it is the same force that acts according to this law throughout nature, it is evident that, the earth being sixty half-diameters distant from the moon, a heavy body falling to the earth must cover fifteen feet in the first second and 54,000 feet in the first minute.

Now, it does happen that a heavy body falls fifteen feet in the first second and in the first minute travels 54,000 feet, which number is the square of sixty multiplied by fifteen, so the weight of bodies is in inverse ratio to the squares of distances, so the same force causes weight on the earth and holds the moon in its orbit.

As it is proved that the moon is drawn towards the earth which is the centre of its own particular movement, it is proved that the earth and the moon are drawn towards the sun, which is the centre of their annual movement.

The other planets must be governed by this general law, and if this law exists these planets must follow the laws discovered by Kepler. All these laws and relationships are indeed adhered to with the utmost accuracy by the planets. Therefore the force of gravity draws all the planets towards the sun, like our own globe. Finally, the reactions of all bodies being proportional to their action, it is certain that the earth is in its turn drawn towards the moon and that the sun is drawn towards both, that each of the satellites of Saturn is drawn towards the other four and the other four towards it, and all five towards Saturn and Saturn towards all of them, that the same applies to Jupiter and that all these globes are drawn towards the sun, which in its turn is drawn towards them.

This force of gravity acts in proportion to the matter contained in the bodies – this is a truth Newton has established by experiments. This new discovery has shown that the sun, centre of all the planets, draws them all in direct proportion to their mass combined with their distance. From there, rising by degrees to knowledge that seemed beyond the human mind, he ventures to calculate the amount of matter in the sun and how much there is in each planet. Thus he shows, by the simple laws of mechanics, that each celestial globe must of necessity be at the place where it is. His one principle of the laws of gravitation explains all the apparent inequalities in the paths of the heavenly bodies. The variations of the moon become a necessary result of these laws. Moreover it is clear why the nodes of the moon take nineteen years to perform a revolution and those of the earth about twenty-six thousand years. The high and low tides of the sea are another very simple effect of this attraction. The proximity of the moon when it is full or when it is new and its greater distance at the quarters, together with the action of the sun, provide a convincing reason for the rise and fall of the ocean.

Having with his sublime theory accounted for the courses and variations of the planets, he applies the same law to the comets. These lights, mysterious for so long, that used to be the terror of the earth and wreck natural science, placed by Aristotle below the moon and by Descartes above Saturn, have at last been put in their rightful place by Newton.

He proves that they are solid bodies which move within the sphere of action of the sun and describe an ellipse which is so eccentric and so resembles a parabola that certain comets must take more than five hundred years to perform a revolution.

Halley believes that the comet of 1680 is the same one that appeared at the time of Julius Caesar. This one especially serves better than any other to show that the comets are hard and opaque bodies, for it descended so near to the sun that it was only one sixth of its disc away. Consequently it must have been heated to a temperature two thousand times hotter than that of the hottest iron. If it had not been an opaque body it would have been dispersed and consumed in no time. Then the fashion began of guessing the paths of the comets. The celebrated mathematician Jacques Bernoulli[22] concluded from his system that the famous comet of 1680 would reappear on 17 May 1719. On that night of 17 May not a single astronomer in Europe went to bed, but the famous comet did not appear. It is at least more astute, though no more certain, to give it 575 years to come back. An English mathematician named Whiston,[23] no less fanciful than mathematical, has seriously affirmed that at the time of the Flood there had been a comet that had inundated our globe, and he was unreasonable enough to be astonished that people laughed at him. Antiquity thought in about the same way as Whiston, and believed that the comets were always the forerunners of some great disaster on the earth. Newton, on the contrary, suspects that they are very beneficial and that the vapours they give off only serve to help and vivify the planets which in their courses take in all the particles the sun has detached from the comets. This opinion is at least more probable than the other.

That is not all. If this force of gravity or attraction acts in all heavenly spheres, it acts no doubt on all the parts of those spheres, for if bodies attract each other in proportion to their masses, it can only be in proportion to the quantity of their parts. And if this power is present in the whole, it certainly is in the half, the quarter, the eighth and so ad infinitum. Moreover if this power were not equally in each part, there would always be certain parts of the globe that would gravitate more than the others, which is not the case. So this power actually exists in all matter, and in the smallest particles of matter.

Thus attraction is the mainspring which keeps the whole of nature in motion.

Newton foresaw clearly when he had demonstrated the existence of this principle that people would revolt against its very name. In more than one place in his book he cautions the reader against gravitation itself and warns him not to confuse it with what the Ancients termed occult qualities, but to be satisfied with the knowledge that there is in all bodies a central force which acts from end to end of the universe on the nearest and most distant bodies in accordance with the changeless laws of mechanics.

It is amazing that after the solemn protestations of this great philosopher, M. Saurin[24] and M. de Fontenelle, who deserve this title themselves, should have accused him clearly of the visions of the Peripatetics: M. Saurin in the Memoirs of the Academy for 1709 and M. de Fontenelle in the *Eulogy of Newton* itself.

Almost all the French, learned or not, have repeated this accusation. On all sides you hear: 'Why didn't Newton use the word impulsion, which we understand so well, rather than the term attraction, which we don't?'

Newton could have replied to his critics: 'Firstly, you no more understand the word impulsion than you do the word attraction, and if you cannot grasp why one body tends towards the centre of another, you cannot imagine any the more by what virtue one body can push another.

'Secondly, I could not admit the term impulsion because to do so I would have had to know that some celestial matter does indeed impel the planets. Now not only have I no knowledge of this matter, but I have proved that it does not exist.

'Thirdly, I only use the word attraction to express an effect I have discovered in nature – a certain and indisputable effect of an unknown principle, a quality inherent in matter the cause of which cleverer men than I will find if they can.'

'Then what have you taught us?' people still insist. 'And why so many calculations to tell us what you don't understand yourself?'

'I have taught you,' Newton could go on, 'that the mechanics of central forces makes all bodies weigh in proportion to their matter, that these central forces alone make the planets and comets move in clearly defined proportions. I show you that it is impossible that there should be any other cause of the weight and movement of all the heavenly bodies, for as heavy bodies fall to the ground in accordance with the known proportion of the central forces, and as the planets move in their courses in these same proportions, if there were yet another force acting on all these bodies it would increase their velocities or change their directions. Now, none of these bodies ever has a single degree of movement, speed or direction not demonstrably the effect of the central forces. So it is impossible that there can be another principle.'

May I be allowed to let Newton speak for another moment. Will he not be justified in saying: 'I am a very different case from the Ancients. They, for example, saw water rise in a pump and said, "The water rises because it abhors a vacuum." But I am like the first man who noticed that water rises in pumps and left to others the task of explaining the cause of this effect. The first anatomist to say that the arms move because the muscles contract taught men an incontestable truth. Shall we be less indebted to him because he did not know the reason why the muscles contract? The cause of the elasticity of the air is unknown, but the man who discovered this spring rendered a great service to physics. The spring I have discovered was less obvious, more universal, so people should be more grateful to me. I have discovered a new property of matter, one of the secrets of the Creator. I have calculated and demonstrated its effects; should people quibble with me over the name I give it?

'It is the vortices that might be called an occult quality, since nobody has ever proved their existence. Attraction on the contrary is a real thing, since its effects can be demonstrated and its proportions calculated. The cause of this cause is in the mind of God.'

Procedes huc, et non ibis amplius.

LETTER 16

*

ON THE OPTICS OF NEWTON

A NEW universe has been discovered by the scientists of the last century, and this new world was all the more difficult to understand because its very existence had not been suspected. It seemed to the wisest that it was temerarious even to dare to think one could guess by what laws the heavenly bodies move and how light works.

Galileo with his astronomical discoveries, Kepler with his calculation, Descartes at least in his dioptrics and Newton in all his works, have seen the mechanism of the working of the world. Mathematics has subjected infinity to calculation. The circulation of the blood in animals and of the sap in plants has changed nature for us. A new kind of existence has been given to bodies by the pneumatic machine, objects have been brought close to our eyes by the help of telescopes, and finally, what Newton has discovered about light matches the most daring exploits human curiosity could expect after so many novelties.

Before Antonio de Dominis[25] the rainbow had seemed to be an inexplicable miracle; this scientist sensed that it was an inevitable effect of rain and sun. Descartes immortalized his name by the mathematical explanation of this quite natural phenomenon; he calculated the reflections of light in the rain-drops, and this sagacity at that time verged on the divine.

But what would he have said had he been told that he was mistaken about the nature of light, that there was no way of being sure that it was a globular body, that it is not true that this matter, spread throughout the universe, only needs to be set in action by a push from the sun, like a long stick that acts at one end when it is pushed at the other, that it is perfectly true that it is flashed by the sun, and finally that light is transmitted from the sun to the earth in roughly seven minutes, although a cannon-ball, keeping its uniform speed, cannot do this journey in under twenty-five years?

What would have been his amazement had he been told: 'It is not true that light is reflected directly by bouncing on the solid parts of a body, nor that bodies are transparent when they have large pores, and a man will come who will demonstrate these paradoxes and dissect a single ray of light with more dexterity than the most skilful surgeon dissects the human body.'

This man has come. Newton, with the help of nothing but the prism, has shown before our very eyes that light is a mixture of coloured rays which together give the colour white. A single ray is divided by him into seven rays which all shine on to a piece of cloth or white paper in their order, one above the other at unequal distances. The first is red, the second orange, the third yellow, the fourth green, the fifth blue, the sixth indigo, the seventh violet. Each of these rays, filtered later through a hundred other prisms, will never change its colour, just as refined gold will never change in crucibles. And by way of superabundant proof that each of these primary rays bears within itself what makes its colour in our eyes, take, for example, a little piece of yellow wood and expose it to the red ray: the wood is immediately tinged with red; expose it to the green ray, it takes the green colour, and so on.

What then is the cause of colour in nature? Nothing more than the aptitude of certain substances for reflecting rays of a certain kind and absorbing all the others. What is this hidden aptitude? He demonstrates that it is solely the thickness of the tiny constituent parts of which a substance is made up. And how does this reflection take place? It was formerly thought because the rays bounced, like a ball, off the surface of a solid body. Not at all. Newton informs astonished scientists that bodies are opaque only because their pores are large, that light is reflected to our eyes from within the pores themselves, and that the smaller the pores the more transparent the body. Thus paper, which reflects light when it is dry, transmits it when greasy because the grease, filling the pores, makes them much smaller.

So, examining the extreme porosity of bodies, each part having its pores and each part of these parts having its own, he shows that there is no certainty that there exists a single cubic inch of solid matter in the universe, so remote is our intelligence from conceiving what matter is!

Having thus decomposed light and carried the brilliance of his discoveries to the point of demonstrating the method of understanding a compound colour by its primary colours, he shows that these basic rays separated by the prism are only arranged in that order because they are refracted in that very order. And it is this property, unknown until his time, of breaking up in that proportion, this unequal refraction of rays, this property of refracting red less than orange, etc. that he calls refrangibility.

The most reflectible rays are the most refrangible; hence he shows that the same property causes the reflection and the refraction of light.

All these marvels are but the beginning of his discoveries; he found the secret of seeing the vibrations and impulses of light, coming and going endlessly, which transmit light or reflect it according to the thickness of the particles they meet. He ventured to calculate the thickness of the particles of air required between two pieces of glass placed one on the other, the one flat and the other convex on one side, in order to produce a certain transmission or reflection and to make such and such a colour.

From all these experiments he finds the proportion in which light acts on bodies and bodies on light.

He understood light so well that he determined how far the art of augmenting it or helping our eyesight with telescopes should go.

Descartes, with a fine and very pardonable confidence in view of the enthusiasm with which he was fired by the early stages of an art almost discovered by him, Descartes hoped, with the aid of telescopes, to see in the heavenly bodies objects as small as those perceived on earth.

Newton has shown that lenses cannot be improved any

further because of this very refraction and refrangibility which, as they bring objects nearer to us separate the primary rays too widely. He has calculated the proportion of separation of red and blue rays in these lenses and, carrying his demonstration into fields the very existence of which was unsuspected, he examines the inequalities produced by the shaping of the lens and the refrangibility. He has found that, the object-glass of the telescope being convex on one side and flat on the other, if the flat side is turned towards the object, the error due to the construction and position of the lens is five thousand times less than the error from refrangibility. Thus it is not because of the shaping of lenses that one cannot perfect telescopes but because the fault lies in the very nature of light.

That is why he invented a telescope that shows objects by reflection and not by refraction. This new kind of telescope is very difficult to make and not very easy to use, but it is said in England that a five-foot reflecting telescope has the same effect as an ordinary one of a hundred feet.

LETTER 17

*

ON INFINITY AND CHRONOLOGY

THE labyrinth and abyss of infinity is another new journey undertaken by Newton and he has given us the thread with which we can find our way through.

Once again Descartes is his predecessor in this astonishing new development; in his mathematics he was moving rapidly towards infinity, but he stopped on the brink. Towards the middle of the last century Wallis was the first to reduce a fraction by recurring division to an infinite series.

Lord Brouncker used this series to square the hyperbola.[26]

Mercator published a demonstration of this squaring. It was at about this time that Newton, at the age of twenty-three, invented a general method of performing with all curves what had been tried on the hyperbola.

It is this method of subjecting the infinite in all cases to algebraical calculation that is called differential calculus, or fluxions, and integral calculus. It is the art of numerating and measuring accurately something the very existence of which cannot be conceived.

And, indeed, wouldn't you think someone is teasing you when he says that there are infinitely long lines that form an infinitely small angle?

Or that a straight line, which is straight as long as it is finite, by changing its direction infinitely little becomes an infinite curve, and that a curve can become infinitely less curved?

That there are squares of infinity, cubes of infinity and infinite infinities, the penultimate of which is nothing in comparison to the last?

All this, which at first seems the very extreme of absurdity, is in reality an effort of the subtlety and breadth of the human mind, and the way of finding truths hitherto unknown.

This most daring edifice is even founded upon simple ideas. It involves measuring the diagonal of a square, ascertaining the area of a curve and finding the square root of a number that has none in ordinary arithmetic.

And after all, so many orders of infinity should no more outrage the imagination than this familiar proposition that between a circle and a tangent it is always possible to pass curves, or again that matter is always divisible. These two truths have long been demonstrated and are no more comprehensible than the others.

For a long time Newton's claim to be the inventor of the famous calculus has been challenged. Leibnitz in Germany has been credited with the invention of the differentials that Newton calls fluxions, and Bernoulli has claimed the integral calculus, but the honour of the first discovery has remained Newton's, leaving the others the glory of having raised a doubt as to whether it was to be theirs or his.

In the same way Harvey's discovery of the circulation of the blood has been contested, and Perrault's of the circulation of sap. Hartsoeker and Leuvenhoeck have each claimed the honour of being the first to have seen the microscopic creatures of which we are made. The same Hartsoeker has disputed Huyghens's invention of a new way of calculating the distance of a fixed star. Nobody knows so far what scientist found the problem of the cycloid.

However that may be, it is through this mathematics of the infinite that Newton reached the most advanced knowledge.

It remains for me to mention another work which is more accessible to men in general but for ever bears witness to the creative spirit Newton carried into all his researches. This is a chronology of quite a new kind, for in everything he undertook he had to change notions accepted by other men.

Accustomed to disentangle chaos, he sought to throw at least some light upon that of ancient fables confused with history and to fix an uncertain chronology. It is a fact that there is no family, city or nation which does not try to push its origins further back. Moreover, the earliest historians are the most negligent about indicating dates. Books were far less common than today and consequently, being less open to criticism, authors deceived people with impunity, and since facts have obviously been made up, it is highly probable that dates have been made up too.

In general it seemed to Newton that the world was five hundred years younger than chronologists made out; he bases his idea on the normal course of nature and astronomical observations.

By the course of nature we mean here the span of each generation of men. The Egyptians were the first to use this unreliable method of counting. When they wanted to write down the beginnings of their history they counted three hundred and forty-one generations from Menes to Sethon, and not having any fixed dates they counted three generations to a hundred years. Thus they reckoned eleven thousand, three hundred and forty years from the reign of Menes to that of Sethon.

The Greeks, before counting by Olympiads, followed the Egyptian method, and even extended slightly the length of the generations, stretching each generation to forty years.

Now in this matter the Egyptians and Greeks were mistaken in their calculations. It is quite true that in the normal course of nature three generations make up about a hundred to a hundred and twenty years, but three reigns come well short of that number of years. It is very clear that in general men live longer than kings reign. So a man setting out to write history without having exact dates and knowing that there were nine kings in a nation's history, will be very wrong if he counts three hundred years for those nine kings. Each generation is about thirty-six years, each reign is about twenty on an average. Take the thirty kings of England from the Conqueror to George I; they reigned for six hundred and forty-eight years which, divided among the thirty kings, gives each one a reign of twenty-one and a half years. Sixty-three kings of France have reigned, on average, about twenty years each. That is the normal course of nature. So the ancients were wrong when they made the duration of reigns about equal to that of generations. They counted too much, so it is right to cut their calculations down a little.

Astronomical observations seem to back up our scientist still more: he seems stronger when he is fighting on his own ground.

You know, Sir, that the earth, in addition to its annual movement which carries it round the sun from west to east in the space of one year, performs another strange revolution quite unknown until recent times. Its poles have a very slow retrogressive movement from east to west, which means that day by day their position does not correspond exactly with the same points in the sky. This difference, imperceptible in one year, becomes quite appreciable with time, and after seventy-two years the difference is found to be of one degree, that is the three hundred and sixtieth part of the whole heavens. So after seventy-two years the colure of the spring equinox, which passed through a fixed point, corresponds to a different fixed point. Hence the sun, instead of being in the part of the sky where the Ram used to be in Hipparchus's time, now corresponds to that part of the sky where Taurus used to be, and Gemini are where Taurus was then. All the Signs have changed places, yet we still cling to the way of speaking of the Ancients; we say that the sun is in the Ram in spring just as we condescend to say that the sun goes round.

Hipparchus[27] was the first of the Greeks to notice changes in the constellations in relation to the equinoxes, or rather to learn it from the Egyptians. Scientists attributed this movement to the stars, for at that time they were very far from imagining such a revolution of the earth, which was believed to be immovable in any direction. So they created a heaven to which they attached all the stars, and gave this sky its own motion, which made it move eastwards while all the stars seemed to follow their daily path from east to west. To this error they added another far more important one; they believed that the supposititious sky of the fixed stars moved eastwards by one degree every hundred years. Thus they were just as wrong in their astronomical calculations as in their physical system. For example, an astronomer would have said at that time: 'The spring equinox, at the time of such and such an observer, was at a certain Sign, a certain star; it has moved two degrees between that observer's time and our own. Now two degrees equal two hundred years, therefore that observer lived two hundred years before me.' It is obvious that an astronomer who reasoned in that way would have been wrong by just fifty-four years. That is why the Ancients, doubly mistaken, made their Great Year, that is to say revolution of the whole sky, about thirty-six thousand years. But the Moderns know that this imaginary revolution of the sky and stars is nothing more than the revolution of the poles of the earth, which takes twenty-five thousand nine hundred years. It is well to note here, incidentally, that Newton, when determining the figure of the earth, very satisfactorily explained the reason for this revolution.

When all that has been stated, in order to establish chronology it remains to be seen through what star the equinoctial colure cuts the spring ecliptic today, and to know whether there is not some Ancient who has told us at what point the ecliptic was cut in his time by the same equinoctial colure.

Clement of Alexandria reports that Chiron, who took part in the expedition of the Argonauts, observed the constellations at the time of that famous expedition, and fixed the spring equinox in the middle of the Ram, the autumn equinox in the middle of Libra, our summer solstice in the middle of Cancer and the winter solstice in the middle of Capricorn.

Long after the Argonauts' expedition and one year before the Peloponnesian war, Meton observed that the point of the summer solstice passed through the eighth degree of Cancer.

Now there are thirty degrees to each Sign of the Zodiac. At the time of Chiron the solstice was at the halfway point of the Sign, that is at the fifteenth degree; one year before the Peloponnesian war it was at the eighth, so it had gone back seven degrees. One degree equals seventy-two years, so from the beginning of the Peloponnesian war to the expedition of the Argonauts there are only seven times seventy-two years, which makes five hundred and four years, and not seven hundred, as the Greeks said. Thus by comparing the state of the heavens today with the state they were in then, we see that the expedition of the Argonauts must be put at about nine hundred years before Christ and not at about fourteen hundred, and consequently the world is about five hundred years younger than used to be thought. Hence all periods are brought closer together and everything happened later than it was said to. I don't know whether this ingenious system will have a brilliant future and whether people will be willing to reshape the chronology of the world along these lines. Perhaps scientists might find it too much to grant the same man the honour of having perfected physics, mathematics and history at the same time; it would be a kind of universal sovereignty difficult for personal pride to accept. So at the time when very distinguished scientists were attacking him on the subject of gravity, others were combating his chronological system. Time, which should show to whom victory is due, will perhaps only leave the dispute more undecided.

LETTER 18

*

ON TRAGEDY

THE English already had a theatre, as did the Spanish, when the French still had nothing but portable stages. Shakespeare, who was considered the English Corneille, flourished at about the time of Lope de Vega. He had a strong and fertile genius, full of naturalness and sublimity, without the slightest spark of good taste or the least knowledge of the rules. I am going to tell you something rash but true, namely that the excellence of this author ruined the English theatre: there are such wonderful scenes, such grand and terrible passages scattered about in his monstrous farces, which are called tragedies, that these plays have always been performed with great success. Time, which alone makes the reputation of men, ends by making their defects respectable. After two hundred years most of the outlandish and monstrous ideas of this author have acquired the right to be considered sublime, and almost all modern authors have copied him. But what succeeded in Shakespeare is booed in them and, as you can imagine, the veneration in which this Ancient is held increases as the Moderns are despised. It does not occur to people that they should not copy him, and the lack of success of their copies simply makes people think that he is inimitable.

You know that in the tragedy of the *Moor of Venice*, a most touching play, a husband strangles his wife on the stage, and while the poor woman is being strangled, she shrieks that she is dying most undeservedly. You are not unaware that in *Hamlet* gravediggers dig a grave, swallowing drinks and singing popular songs, cracking jokes typical of men of their calling about the skulls they come across. But what will surprise you is that these stupidities should have been imitated in the reign of Charles II, which was the age of politeness and the golden age of the arts.

Otway,[28] in his *Venice Preserv'd*, introduces Senator Antonio and the courtesan Naki amid the horrors of the conspiracy of the Marquis of Bedmar. Old Senator Antonio with his courtesan goes through all the monkey tricks of an old debauchee who is impotent and out of his mind; he pretends to be a bull and a dog, he bites his mistress's legs and she kicks and whips him. These buffooneries, catering for the dregs of society, have been cut from Otway's play, but in Shakespeare's *Julius Caesar* the jokes of Roman shoemakers and cobblers, introduced on the stage with Brutus and Cassius, have been left in. That is because the stupidity of Otway is modern, while Shakespeare's is ancient.

You may well complain that those who have discussed the English theatre up to now, and above all the famous Shakespeare, have so far only pointed out his errors, and that nobody has translated any of the striking passages which atone for all his faults. I will answer that it is very easy to set out the errors of a poet in prose but very difficult to translate his beautiful lines. All the scribblers who set themselves up as critics of celebrated authors compile volumes. I would prefer two pages that pointed out a few of the beauties. For I shall always hold, with men of good taste, that there is more to be gained from a dozen lines of Homer and Virgil than from all the criticisms that have ever been written about these two great men.

I have ventured to translate a few passages of the best English poets. Here is one from Shakespeare. Have pity on the copy for the sake of the original, and always bear in mind when you see a translation that you are only looking at a feeble print of a great picture.

I have chosen the monologue from the tragedy of *Hamlet* which is familiar to all and begins with this line:

> To be or not to be, that is the question.

It is Hamlet, prince of Denmark, speaking:

> *Demeure; il faut choisir, et passer à l'instant*
> *De la vie à la mort, ou de l'être au néant.*

Dieux cruels! s'il en est, éclairez mon courage.
Faut-il vieillir courbé sous la main qui m'outrage,
Supporter ou finir mon malheur et mon sort?
Qui suis-je? qui m'arrête? et qu'est-ce que la mort?
C'est la fin de nos maux, c'est mon unique asile;
Après de longs transports, c'est un sommeil tranquille;
On s'endort, et tout meurt. Mais un affreux réveil
Doit succéder peut-être aux douceurs du sommeil.
On nous menace, on dit que cette courte vie
De tourments éternels est aussitôt suivie.
O mort! moment fatal! affreuse éternité!
Tout coeur à ton seul nom se glace, épouvanté.
Eh! qui pourrait sans toi supporter cette vie,
De nos Prêtres menteurs bénir l'hypocrisie,
D'une indigne maîtresse encenser les erreurs,
Ramper sous un Ministre, adorer ses hauteurs,
Et montrer les langueurs de son âme abattue
A des amis ingrats qui détournent la vue?
La mort serait trop douce en ces extrémités;
Mais le scrupule parle, et nous crie: 'Arrêtez.'
Il défend à nos mains cet heureux homicide,
Et d'un Héros guerrier fait un chrétien timide, etc

Do not suppose that I have rendered the English word for word; woe to the makers of literal translations, who by rendering every word weaken the meaning! It is indeed by so doing that we can say the letter kills and the spirit gives life.

Here is another passage from a famous English tragic poet, Dryden, a poet of the time of Charles II, more productive than wise, whose reputation would have been unblemished had he only produced a tenth part of his works, and whose great drawback is a desire to be universal.

The passage begins thus:

When I consider life, 'tis all a cheat.
Yet fool'd by hope men favour the deceit.

De desseins en regrets et d'erreurs en désirs
Les mortels insensés promènent leur folie.
Dans des malheurs présents, dans l'espoir des plaisirs,
Nous ne vivons jamais, nous attendons la vie.

Demain, demain, dit-on, va combler tous nos voeux;
Demain vient, et nous laisse encore plus malheureux.
Quelle est l'erreur, hélas! du soin qui nous dévore?
Nul de nous ne voudrait recommencer son cours:
De nos premiers moments nous maudissons l'aurore,
Et de la nuit qui vient nous attendons encore
Ce qu'ont en vain promis les plus beaux de noss jours, etc

It is in these isolated passages that English tragic writers have excelled so far. Their plays, almost all barbarous, quite lacking in good taste, order and plausibility, have amazing flashes amid this gloom. The style is too bombastic, too far removed from nature, too much copied from Hebrew writers who are themselves so full of Asiatic hot air. But also it must be admitted that the stilts of the figurative style upon which the English language is raised do lift the spirit very high, although with an irregular gait.

The first Englishman to create a reasonable play written from end to end with elegance is the illustrious Addison. His *Cato of Utica* is a masterpiece in diction and beauty of verse. The role of Cato is to my mind far superior to that of Cornélie in Corneille's *Pompée*, for Cato is great without being high-flown, while Cornélie, who in any case is not an essential character, sometimes goes in for talking riddles. Addison's Cato seems to me the finest character on any stage, but the other characters in the play do not come up to him, and this work, though so well written, is marred by a frigid love plot which casts a mortal languor over the play.

The custom of dragging love somehow or other into dramatic works travelled from Paris to London in about 1660, with our ribbons and our perukes. Women, who adorn theatrical performances as they do here, will not abide that anything else but love be discussed in front of them. The astute Addison was weak and complaisant enough to bend the austerity of his character to fit the manners of his age, and spoiled a masterpiece through anxiety to please.

Since him plays have become more regular, people harder to please and authors more correct and less outrageous. I have seen recent plays very regular but frigid. It seems as though up to now the English have been born to create only irregular things of beauty. The brilliant monstrosities of Shakespeare are a thousand times more pleasing than modern conventionality. Until now the English poetic genius has been like an unruly tree planted by nature, throwing a thousand branches in all directions and growing irregularly but vigorously. It dies if you seek to force its nature and trim it like one of the trees in the gardens of Marly.

LETTER 19

*

ON COMEDY

I DON'T know how the wise and ingenious M. de Muralt,[29] whose *Lettres sur les Anglais et sur les Français* we possess, restricted himself, when discussing comedy, to criticizing a comic writer named Shadwell. This author was pretty well looked down on in his own time; he was not the poet of the best people, his plays, enjoyed for a few performances by the mob, were scorned by all men of taste and resembled so many plays I have seen in France which drew the crowds and offended readers, of which it could be said: *Tout Paris les condamne, et tout Paris les court.*

M. de Muralt ought, I feel, to have told us about an excellent author who lived at that time, namely Mr Wicherley[30] [*sic*], who was for a long time the acknowledged lover of the most illustrious mistress of Charles II. This man, who moved in the highest society, knew all about its vices and absurdities and painted them with the most firm hand and in the truest colours.

He created a misanthrope, imitated from Molière. All the strokes in Wicherley are clearer and bolder than those of our misanthrope, but also less delicate and less circumspect. The English author has corrected the only weakness in the Molière play, which is lack of plot and sustained interest. The English play is interesting and its plot ingenious, though it is perhaps too crude for our taste. It is about a sea captain, full of valour, straightforwardness and scorn for the human race; he has a wise and true friend whom he mistrusts, and a mistress whom he doesn't deign to look at, although she loves him dearly. On the contrary he has pinned all his faith on a false friend who is the most despicable man alive, and has given his heart to the most flighty and disloyal of women. He is quite sure that this woman is a Penelope and the false friend a Cato. He goes off to fight the Dutch, leaving all his money, his jewellery and everything he possesses with this paragon, and recommends the woman herself to this faithful friend whom he trusts so implicitly. Meanwhile the really good man whom he so much mistrusts embarks with him, and the lady whom he has not even deigned to look at disguises herself as a page and makes the trip, without the captain discovering her sex throughout the campaign.

Having got his ship blown up in a fight, the captain returns to London with no resources, no ship and no money, together with his page and his friend, unaware of the friendship of the one and the love of the other. He makes at once for the pearl among women, expecting to find her with his cash-box and her loyalty. He finds her married to the honest rogue in whom he had put his trust, and they have no more kept his money than anything else. Our man finds it the most difficult thing in the world to believe that an honest woman can play such tricks, but to convince him still more this virtuous dame falls in love with the young page and tries to take him by force. But as justice has to be done, and in a play wickedness has to be punished and virtue rewarded, it works out in the end that the captain takes the place of the page, sleeps with the faithless woman, cuckolds his treacherous friend and runs a sword through his body, recovers his cash-box and marries his page. Note that in addition this play is also livened up with a Widow Blackacre, a litigious old girl related to the captain, who is the most amusing creature and the most excellent theatre.

Wicherley also drew upon Molière for a play no less unusual and no less daring: a kind of *École des Femmes*.

The principal character in the play is a lady-killer, the terror of London husbands who, to be more sure of his object, hits on the idea of spreading the rumour that during his recent illness the surgeon found it advisable to make him a eunuch. With that fine reputation all the husbands come to him with their wives, and the poor fellow's only embarrassment is the choice. He looks with the greatest favour upon a little countrywoman with a lot of innocence and voluptuousness, who cuckolds her husband with a candour much more worthwhile than the antics of the most expert ladies. This play is not what you would call the school for good behaviour, but it is indeed the school for wit and good fun.

A Sir John Vanbrugh has written some even more amusing but less ingenious comedies. This Sir John was a man about town as well as a poet and architect; it is affirmed that he wrote as he built, rather clumsily. It was he who built the famous palace of Blenheim as a weighty and durable monument to our unhappy battle of Hochstadt. If only the apartments were as spacious as the walls are thick, this palace would be quite convenient.

Somebody put in Vanbrugh's epitaph that *it was to be hoped that the earth would not lie light on him, since in his lifetime he had weighed it down so inhumanly.*

This knight, having toured France before the war of 1701, was put in the Bastille, where he remained for some time without ever knowing what had brought upon him this mark of distinction on the part of our Government. He wrote a comedy in the Bastille, and what is very strange in my opinion is that there is not a single word in it against the country in which he underwent this violent treatment.

Of all the English, the one who carried the glory of the comic theatre to the greatest heights is the late Mr Congreve. He only wrote a few plays but they are all excellent of their kind. The rules of the theatre are rigorously observed; the plays are full of characters differentiated with extreme subtlety, you don't encounter the slightest coarse joke, everywhere you find the language of well-mannered people with the actions of rogues, which proves that he knew his world and lived in what is called good society. When I met him he was infirm and almost at death's door; he had one failing, which was that he did not rank high enough his first profession, that of a writer, which had made his reputation and fortune. He spoke of his works as trifles beneath him, and in our first conversation he told me to think of him as a gentleman who lived very simply. I answered him that if he had had the misfortune of being just a gentleman like any other I would never have come to see him, and I was very shocked at such misplaced vanity.

His plays are the most witty and true to life, those of Vanbrugh the funniest, those of Wicherley the most daring.

It is noteworthy that none of these clever men said anything against Molière. Only bad English authors have decried that great man. It is third-rate Italian musicians who look down on Lully, but a Bononcini admires him and does him justice, just as a Mead respects a Helvetius and a Silva.

England has other good comic writers such as Sir Richard Steele and Mr Cibber, an excellent actor and also Poet Laureate, a title that seems ridiculous but which does provide an income of a thousand *écus* and some worthwhile privileges. Our great Corneille did not get as much.

For the rest, don't ask me to go into any detail about these English plays of which I am such a champion, nor to report a witticism or joke of Wicherley or Congreve; humour cannot be translated. If you want to understand English comedy there is no other way but to go to London, stay there three years, learn English properly and go to the play every day. I don't get much pleasure from reading Plautus and Aristophanes – why? Because I am neither Greek nor Roman. The subtleties of verbal quips, allusions, topicality are all lost on a foreigner.

This is not the same in Tragedy. In tragedy it is only a matter of great passions and heroic nonsense hallowed by ancient errors of fable or history. *Oedipus, Electra* belong as much to the Spaniards, the English and ourselves as to the Greeks. But good comedy is the speaking image of the absurdities of a nation, and if you don't know the nation inside out you can hardly judge the portrait.

LETTER 20

*

ON NOBLE LORDS WHO CULTIVATE
LITERATURE

THERE was a time in France when the fine arts were cultivated by the highest in the land. The courtiers in particular were interested in spite of the dissipation, the taste for trifles, the passion for intrigue which held divine sway in the country.

It seems to me that at the present time the taste at Court is far removed from letters. Perhaps in a short time the fashion for using one's mind will come back – a king has only to have the will and he makes what he likes of a nation. In England as a rule people think, and literature is more honoured than in France. This advantage is a natural outcome of the form of their government. In London there are some eight hundred people with the right to speak in public and uphold the interests of the nation; about five or six thousand aspire to the same honour in their turn, all the rest set themselves up in judgement on these, and anybody can print what he thinks about public affairs. So the whole nation is obliged to study. One hears nothing but talk of the governments of Athens and Rome, and so willy-nilly one has to read the authors who have dealt with them, and this study leads naturally to literature. In general men have the intellectual capacity for their job. Why do our magistrates, lawyers, doctors and many priests usually have more literary ability, taste and intelligence than are found in all the other professions? Because their profession really is to possess a cultivated mind, just as that of a business man is to know his business. Not long ago a very young English lord came to see me in Paris on his way home from Italy.[31] He had written a description of that country in verse with as much elegance as anything done by the Earl of Rochester[32] and our Chaulieu, Sarrasin or Chapelle.

The translation I have done of it is so far from reaching the vigour and humour of the original that I am obliged to ask very seriously the forgiveness of the author, and of those who understand English. However, as I have no other way of introducing Lord X's verses, here they are in my own language:

> Qu'ai-je donc vu dans l'Italie?
> Orgueil, astuce et pauvreté,
> Grands compliments, peu de bonté,
> Et beaucoup de cérémonie;
> L'extravagante comédie
> Que souvent l'Inquisition*
> Veut qu'on nomme religion,
> Mais qu'ici nous nommons folie.
> La nature, en vain bienfaisante,
> Veut enrichir ces lieux charmants;
> Des prêtres la main désolante
> Étouffe ses plus beaux présents.
> Les Monsignors, soi-disant grands,
> Seuls dans leurs palais magnifiques,
> Y sont d'illustres fainéants,
> Sans argent et sans domestiques.
> Pour les petits, sans liberté,
> Martyrs du joug qui les domine,
> Ils ont fait voeu de pauvreté,
> Priant Dieu par oisiveté,
> Et toujours jeûnant par famine.
> Ces beaux lieux, du Pape bénis,
> Semblent habités par les diables,
> Et les habitants misérables
> Sont damnés dans le paradis.

Perhaps it will be said that these lines are written by a heretic, but we translate every day, and often rather badly, those of Horace and Juvenal, who had the misfortune to be heathens. You realize that a translator cannot be held responsible for the sentiments of his author; all he can do is to pray to God for his conversion, and that I shall not fail to do for his Lordship's.

*No doubt he means the farces that certain preachers go through in public places. [Voltaire's own note.]

ON THE EARL OF ROCHESTER AND
MR WALLER[33]

EVERYBODY has heard of the Earl of Rochester. M. de Saint-Evremond[34] has said a great deal about him, but he has only told us about the celebrated Rochester as a man of pleasure, a man about town. I want to introduce the man of genius and great poet. Among other brilliant works of this dazzling imagination which belonged to him alone, he wrote several satires on the same subjects as our celebrated Despréaux had chosen. I can think of nothing more beneficial, for perfecting one's taste, than the comparison of great geniuses who have worked on the same subjects.

This is how M. Despréaux speaks against human reason in his satire on man:

> *Cependant, à le voir, plein de vapeurs légères,*
> *Soi-même se bercer de ses propres chimères,*
> *Lui seul de la nature est la base et l'appui,*
> *Et le dixième Ciel ne tourne que pour lui.*
> *De tous les animaux il est ici le maître;*
> *Qui pourrait le nier, poursuis-tu? Moi, peut-être:*
> *Ce maître prétendu qui leur donne des lois,*
> *Ce Roi des animaux, combien a-t-il de Rois?*

This is roughly how the Earl of Rochester expresses himself in his satire on man, but the reader must always bear in mind that these are free renderings of English poets, and that the trammels of our versification and the delicate susceptibilities of our language cannot give the equivalent of the impetuous freedom of English style:

> *Cet esprit que je hais, cet esprit plein d'erreur,*
> *Ce n'est pas ma raison, c'est la tienne, Docteur;*
> *C'est ta raison frivole, inquiète, orgueilleuse,*

Des sages animaux rivale dédaigneuse,
Qui croit entre eux et l'Ange occuper le milieu,
Et pense être ici-bas l'image de son Dieu,
Vil atome importun, qui croit, doute, dispute,
Rampe, s'élève, tombe, et nie encor sa chute;
Qui nous dit: 'Je suis libre', en nous montrant ses fers,
Et dont l'oeil trouble et faux croit percer l'Univers,
Allez, révérends fous, bienheureux fanatiques!
Compilez bien l'amas de vos riens scolastiques!
Pères de visions et d'énigmes sacrés,
Auteurs du labyrinthe où vous vous égarez,
Allez obscurément éclaircir vos mystères,
Et courez dans l'école adorer vos chimères!
Il est d'autres erreurs; il est de ces dévots,
Condamnés par eux-mêmes à l'ennui du repos.
Ce mystique encloîtré, fier de son indolence,
Tranquille au sein de Dieu, qu'y peut-il faire? Il pense.
Non, tu ne penses point, misérable, tu dors,
Inutile à la terre et mis au rang des morts;
Ton esprit énervé croupit dans la mollesse;
Réveille-toi, sois homme, et sors de ton ivresse.
L'homme est né pour agir, et tu prétends penser!

Whether these ideas be true or false, it is at any rate certain that they are expressed with the energy which makes a poet.

I shall take care not to examine the matter philosophically, nor to exchange the brush for the compass. My only object in this letter is to point out the genius of the English poets, and I shall continue in this tone.

Much has been said in France about the celebrated Waller. La Fontaine, Saint-Evremond and Bayle[35] have sung his praises, but all that is known of him is his name. He had about the same reputation in London as Voiture[36] in Paris, and I think he was more worthy of it. Voiture came at a time when we were emerging from barbarism and were still in ignorance. Everybody wanted to be a wit, but nobody yet had any wit. We sought turns of expression instead of thoughts; artificial jewels are easier to find than precious stones. Voiture, born with a frivolous and facile talent, was the first to shine in this dawn of

French literature. Had he come after the great men who adorned the age of Louis XIV, either he would have been unknown, or he would only have been mentioned with contempt, or he would have corrected his style. M. Despréaux praises him, but only in his earliest satires, when his own taste was not yet formed. He was young, in an age when one judges men by their reputation and not for themselves. Besides, Despréaux was often very unfair in his praises and censures. He praised Segrais, whom nobody reads, he insulted Quinault, whom everybody knows by heart, and he says nothing about La Fontaine. Waller, though better than Voiture, was not yet perfect; his love poems breathe an air of grace, but carelessness makes them falter and often they are disfigured by ideas that ring false. In his time the English had not yet reached the stage of writing correctly. His serious works are full of a vigour quite unexpected after the languor of his other pieces. He wrote a funeral eulogy on Cromwell which, for all its faults, passes for a masterpiece. In order to understand this work it must be borne in mind that on the day Cromwell died a terrible storm was raging.

The piece begins thus:

> Il n'est plus; c'en est fait; soumettons-nous au sort:
> Le ciel a signalé ce jour par des tempêtes,
> Et la voix du tonnerre, éclatant sur nos têtes,
>   Vient d'annoncer sa mort.
> Par ses derniers soupirs il ébranle cette île,
> Cette île que son bras fit trembler tant de fois,
>   Quand, dans le cours de ses exploits,
>   Il brisait la tête des rois
> Et soumettait un peuple à son joug seul docile.
> Mer, tu t'en es troublée. O mer! tes flots émus
> Semblent dire en grondant aux plus lointains rivages
> Que l'effroi de la terre, et ton maître, n'est plus.
> Tel au Ciel autrefois s'envola Romulus,
> Tel il quitta la terre au milieu des orages,
> Tel d'un peuple guerrier il reçut les hommages:
> Obéi dans sa vie, à sa mort adoré,
> Son palais fut un temple, etc.

It is in connection with this eulogy of Cromwell that Waller made this reply to Charles II, which can be found in Bayle's Dictionary. The King, for whom Waller, following the custom of kings and poets, had produced a piece stuffed with praises, reproached him for having done better by Cromwell. Waller replied: 'Sire, we poets do better in fiction than in truth.' This answer was not as sincere as that of the Dutch ambassador who, when the same King complained that people showed less respect for him than for Cromwell, answered: 'Oh, Sire, Cromwell was quite a different kind of man!'

My object is not to write a commentary on the character of Waller or anybody else; after their death I only judge people by their works and for me all the rest counts as nought. I will only remark that Waller, born at Court with an income of sixty thousand *livres*, never had the stupid pride or the indifference to give up his talent. The Earls of Dorset and Roscommon, the two Dukes of Buckingham, Lord Halifax[37] and many others did not feel they were lowering themselves by becoming very great poets and distinguished writers. Their works do them more honour than their names. They cultivated literature just as though they hoped to make their fortunes out of it, and what is more they have made the arts respectable in the eyes of the people, who in all things need to be led by the great, but who in truth model themselves on them less in England than in any other place in the world.

LETTER 22

*

ON MR POPE AND SOME OTHER
FAMOUS POETS

I WANTED to tell you about Mr Prior, one of the most agreeable English poets, whom you knew in Paris as Plenipotentiary and Envoy Extraordinary in 1712. I thought also of giving you some idea of the poems of Lord Roscommon, Lord Dorset, etc., but I feel that I should have to write a long book and that after a great deal of effort I should only give you a very imperfect idea of all these works. Poetry is a kind of music; you must hear it in order to judge. When I translate for you a few passages of these foreign poems I am imperfectly setting down their musical notation, but I cannot express the quality of their songs.

There is one English poem especially that I despaired of introducing you to; it is called *Hudibras*.[38] The subject is the Civil War and the Puritans turned to ridicule. It is like *Don Quixote* and our own *Satire Menippée* run together. Of all the books I have ever read, it is the one in which I have found the most wit, but it is also the most untranslatable. Who would believe that a book that seizes all the ridiculous quirks of mankind and has more ideas than words cannot bear translation? It is because almost everything alludes to particular incidents: most of the ridicule falls on the theologians, and few ordinary people understand that, for it would need a running commentary, and a joke explained ceases to be a joke. Any commentator of *bons mots* is a fool.

That is why the books of the ingenious Dr Swift,[39] called the English Rabelais, will never be properly understood in France. He has the honour of being a priest, like Rabelais, and of mocking everything, like Rabelais, but it does him a great disservice, in my humble opinion, to call him by that name.

Rabelais, in his extravagant and incomprehensible book, manifested extreme gaiety and even greater impertinence; he was lavish with erudition, obscenities and boredom – a good story in two pages at the expense of volumes of rubbish. Only a few people of peculiar taste fancy themselves able to understand and appreciate the whole of this work; the rest of the nation laughs at Rabelais' jokes and despises the book. He is looked upon as the first of the clowns, and people are sorry that a man with so much intelligence put it to such miserable use. He is a drunken philosopher who only wrote when he was drunk.

Swift is a sensible Rabelais living in civilized society. He lacks, it is true, the gaiety of the earlier writer, but he has all the finesse, reason, discrimination and good taste lacking in our Curé of Meudon. His poems have a strange and almost inimitable flavour, he is full of good fun in verse and prose alike, but to understand him you must travel a bit in his country.

You can much more easily form some idea of Pope who is, I think, the most elegant, the most correct and, what is much more, the most musical poet England has ever had. He has reduced the harsh blarings of the English trumpet to the soft sounds of the flute; he can be translated because he is extremely clear, and his subjects are usually general and applicable to all nations.

His *Essay on Criticism* will soon be known in France through the verse translation now being done by the abbé du Resnel.

Here is a passage from his poem *The Rape of the Lock* that I have translated with my usual freedom, for once again I know of nothing worse than translating a poem word for word.

> *Umbriel à l'instant, vieux Gnome rechigné,*
> *Va, d'une aile pesante et d'un air renfrogué,*
> *Chercher, en murmurant, la caverne profonde*
> *Où, loin des doux rayons que répand l'oeil du monde,*
> *La Déesse aux vapeurs a choisi son séjour.*
> *Les tristes Aquilons y sifflent à l'entour,*
> *Et le souffle malsain de leur aride haleine*
> *Y porte aux environs la fièvre et la migraine.*
> *Sur un riche sofa, derrière un paravent,*

Loin des flambeaux, du bruit, des parleurs et du vent,
La quinteuse Déesse incessamment repose,
Le coeur gros de chagrins, sans en savoir la cause,
N'ayant pensé jamais, l'esprit toujours troublé,
L'oeil chargé, le teint pâle et l'hypocondre enflé.
La médisante envie est assise auprès d'elle,
Vieux spectre féminin, décrépite pucelle,
Avec un air dévot déchirant son prochain,
Et chansonnant les gens l'Evangile à la main.
Sur un lit plein de fleurs négligemment penchée,
Une jeune beauté non loin d'elle est couchée:
C'est l'Affectation, qui grasseye en parlant,
Écoute sans entendre, et lorgne en regardant,
Qui rougit sans pudeur, et rit de tout sans joie,
De cent maux différents prétend qu'elle est la proie,
Et, pleine de santé sous le rouge et le fard,
Se plaint avec mollesse, et se pâme avec art.

If you were to read this piece in the original instead of in this feeble translation, you would liken it to the description of La Mollesse in *Le Lutrin*.⁴⁰

I have given you a reasonable treatment of the English poets. I have given you a word or two about their philosophers. As for good historians, I have not met any so far; their history has had to be written by a Frenchman. Possibly the English genius, which is either cool or impetuous, has not yet mastered the unaffected eloquence and noble, simple style of history; possibly, also, party spirit, which distorts the vision, has discredited all their historians: one half of the nation is always the enemy of the other. I have found people who have assured me that the Duke of Marlborough was a coward and that Mr Pope was a fool, just as in France some Jesuits think Pascal was a man of little intelligence and some Jansenists say that Fr Bourdaloue was only a gossip. Mary Stuart is a saintly heroine for Jacobites, for others she is a debauchee, an adulteress and a murderess. Thus in England there are polemics and not history. It is true that there is at present a Mr Gordon, an excellent translator of Tacitus and quite capable of writing the history of his own country, but M. Rapin de Thoyras has forestalled him. At all events it seems to me that the English have no historians as good as ours, no real tragedies but charming comedies, admirable passages of poetry and philosophers who should be the teachers of the human race.

The English have greatly benefited from works in our language, and we in our turn, having lent them so much, should borrow back. The English and ourselves only came after the Italians, who have been our masters in everything and whom we have surpassed in some ways. I don't know to which of the three nations preference should be given, but happy is the man who can appreciate their different merits!

LETTER 23

*

ON THE CONSIDERATION DUE TO
MEN OF LETTERS

NEITHER in England nor any other country in the world can one find such establishments to encourage the arts as in France. There are universities almost everywhere, but it is in France alone that such useful encouragements for astronomy, all branches of mathematics, medicine, antiquarian researches, painting, sculpture and architecture can be found. Louis XIV immortalized himself by all these foundations, and this immortality cost him less than two hundred thousand francs a year.

I must say that one of the things that astonish me is that the English Parliament, which has taken it into its head to promise twenty thousand guineas to whoever does the impossible and discovers the longitudes, has never thought of imitating Louis XIV in his munificence towards the arts.

It is true that in England merit finds other rewards that do the nation more honour. Such is the respect this nation has for talent that a man of parts always makes his fortune there. In France Mr Addison would have been a member of some Academy and might have obtained, through some woman's influence, a pension of twelve hundred *livres*, or more likely he would have got into trouble because someone had noticed in his tragedy *Cato* certain remarks against the doorkeeper of some highly-placed person. In England he has been a Secretary of State. Newton was Master of the Royal Mint, Congreve held an important office, Prior was a Plenipotentiary, Dr Swift is an Irish Dean, and in Ireland he is much more highly thought of than the Primate. If Mr Pope's religion excludes him from office at any rate it does not prevent his translation of Homer from bringing him two hundred thousand francs. For a long time in France I saw the author of *Rhadamisthe*[41] almost dying of starvation, and the son of one of the greatest men France has produced, who was beginning to follow in his father's footsteps, would have been reduced to penury but for M. Fagon.[42] What most encourages the arts in England is the consideration they enjoy; the portrait of the Prime Minister is over the mantelpiece of his room, but I have seen Mr Pope's in a score of houses.

Newton was honoured in his lifetime and after his death, as was justly due. The highest in the land vied with each other for the honour of being pall-bearers at his funeral. Go into Westminster Abbey. It is not the tombs of kings that one admires, but the monuments erected by a grateful nation to the greatest men who have contributed to her glory. There you will see their statues as in Athens one saw those of Sophocles or Plato, and I am persuaded that the sight of these glorious monuments alone has kindled more than one spirit and formed more than one great man.

The English have even been reproached for going too far in the honours they award to mere merit. They have been criticized for burying in Westminster Abbey the famous actress Mrs Oldfield with nearly the same honours that were paid to Newton. It has been suggested by some that they had affected to honour the memory of an actress to this extent in order to make us appreciate still more the barbarous injustice they reproach us with, namely of having thrown the body of Mlle Lecouvreur on to the garbage heap.[43]

But I can assure you that in the funeral of Mrs Oldfield, interred in their Saint-Denis, the English consulted nothing but their taste; they are very far from finding infamy in the art of a Sophocles or a Euripedes and from excluding from the body of their citizens those who devote themselves to declaiming in front of them works that are the pride of their nation.

In the time of Charles I and the early days of the civil wars let loose by rigid fanatics, who in the end were themselves the sufferers, much was written against stage plays, especially since Charles I and his wife, daughter of our Henry the Great, were extremely fond of them.

A doctor named Prynne,[44] scrupulous in the extreme, who would have thought himself damned for ever if he had worn a cassock instead of a short coat, and would have liked one half of the human race to massacre the other for the glory of God and *propaganda fide*, took it into his head to write a very bad book against some quite good comedies that were being played every day perfectly innocently before the King and Queen. He quoted the authority of the Rabbis and some passages in St Bonaventura to prove that the *Oedipus* of Sophocles was the work of the Evil One, that Terence was excommunicated *ipso facto*, and added that doubtless Brutus, who was a very austere Jansenist, had only assassinated Caesar because Caesar, who was High Priest, had composed a tragedy of *Oedipus*. In fact he said that all who went to see a play were excommunicates who abjured their anointing and their baptism. This was an outrage to the King and all the Royal Family. At that stage the English respected Charles I, and they would not endure any talk of excommunicating the very same prince whose head they would cut off later. Mr Prynne was hauled before the Star Chamber, condemned to see his fine book burned by the public hangman and himself to have his ears cut off. His trial can be seen in the public records.

In Italy they take care not to disparage opera and excommunicate Signor Senesino or Signora Cuzzoni.[45] As for me, I would venture to wish that it were possible to suppress in France some wretched books published against our theatres, for when the Italians and the English find that we brand as the greatest infamy an art in which we excel, that we condemn as impious a spectacle acted in monasteries and convents, that we despise plays in which Louis XIV and Louis XV have acted, that we declare to be works of the devil plays approved by the severest magistrates and acted before a virtuous Queen, when, I say, foreigners learn about such impudence, such lack of respect for royal authority, such Gothic barbarism that people dare to call Christian austerity, what do you expect them to think of our nation? And how can they conceive either that our laws sanction an art declared so infamous or that we dare to stigmatize with such infamy an art authorized by the laws, rewarded by the sovereigns, cultivated by the most distinguished men and admired by other nations, and that in the same bookshop can be found the diatribe by Père Le Brun against our theatres side by side with the immortal works of Racine, Corneille, Molière, etc.?

LETTER 24

*

ON ACADEMIES

THE English had an Academy of Science long before us, but it is not as well regulated as ours, probably for the simple reason that it is the older, for if it had been established after the Academy in Paris it would have adopted some of its wise rules and perfected others.

The Royal Society of London lacks the two things most necessary to men: rewards and rules. In Paris membership of the Academy means a guaranteed small fortune for a mathematician or chemist; on the contrary, it costs money to belong to the Royal Society. In England whoever says: 'I love the arts', and wants to be a member of the Society becomes one straight away. But in France to be a member of the Academy and recipient of an income from it, it is not enough to be an enthusiast, one must be a scientist and compete for the position against rival claimants all the more dangerous because they are inspired by a sense of pride, self-interest and by the difficulty itself, and by that inflexibility of mind that usually comes from the persistent study of the mathematical sciences.

The Académie des Sciences is wisely limited to the study of nature, and indeed that is a wide enough field to occupy fifty or sixty people. Its London counterpart mingles literature and science indiscriminately. It seems to me better to have a specialized academy for literature, so that there is no confusion, so that one doesn't see a dissertation on the hair-styles of Roman ladies side by side with a hundred new curves.

Since the Royal Society of London has little order and no encouragement, and that of Paris is on a quite different footing, it is not surprising that the Memoirs of our Academy are superior to theirs: well disciplined and well paid troops must in the long run be better than volunteers. It is true that the

Royal Society had a Newton, but it did not produce him, and, in fact, few of his fellow members understood him; a genius like Newton belonged to all the Academies in Europe, because they all had much to learn from him.

In the last years of the reign of Queen Anne the famous Dr Swift had a plan to set up an academy for the English language, following the example of the Académie Française. This project was supported by the Earl of Oxford, Lord High Treasurer, and even more enthusiastically by Viscount Bolingbroke, Secretary of State, who had the gift of speaking extempore in Parliament with as much purity of style as Swift wrote in his study, and who would have been the patron and the ornament of this Academy. The members who were to have composed it were men whose works will endure as long as the English language: Dr Swift, Mr Prior, whom we have seen as a Minister and who has the same reputation in England as La Fontaine has with us, Mr Pope, the English Boileau, Mr Congreve, who might be called their Molière, and some others whose names escape me now. All these would have made this body flourish at the outset. But the Queen died suddenly, the Whigs took it into their heads to hang all the patrons of the Academy, which, as you may well imagine, was fatal to literature. The members of this body would have had a great advantage over the first ones to make up the Académie Française, for Swift, Prior, Congreve, Dryden, Pope, Addison, etc. had stabilized the English language by their writings, whereas Chapelain, Colletet, Cassaigne, Faret, Perrin, Cotin, your first Academicians were the disgrace of your nation and their names have become so ridiculous that if some passable author had the misfortune to be called Chapelain or Cotin he would have to change his name. Above all, the English Academy would have had to have quite different aims from ours. One day a wit in that country asked me for the Memoirs of the Académie Française. 'It doesn't write memoirs,' I answered, 'but it has printed sixty or eighty volumes of complimentary addresses.' He ran his eye down one or two and could never understand this style, although he understood our good authors perfectly well. 'All I can make out,' he said, 'in these fine discourses is that the member elect, having affirmed that his predecessor was a great man, the Cardinal de Richelieu was a very great man, Chancellor Séguier a fairly great man, Louis XIV more than a great man, the Director replies in the same way and adds that the member elect might also be a sort of great man, and that as for himself, the Director, he does not decline his own share.'

It is easy to see why inevitably almost all these speeches have done so little honour to this body: *vitium est temporis potius quam hominis*. The custom has imperceptibly established itself that every Academician should repeat these eulogies at his reception; it has been a kind of law to bore the public. If you then wonder why the greatest geniuses who have entered this body have sometimes delivered the worst harangues, the reason for that is also very simple; it is that they have wanted to shine by seeking to treat worn-out matter in a new way. The obligation to speak, the awkwardness of having nothing to say and the desire to be brilliant are three things calculated to make even the greatest man ridiculous. Unable to find new ideas they have hunted for new turns of expression, talked without thinking, like people chewing on nothing and giving the appearance of eating while dying of starvation.

Instead of there being a law in the Académie Française to print all these addresses, by which alone it is known, there ought to be a law not to print them.

The Académie des Belles-Lettres has set before itself a wiser and more useful object: to present to the public a collection of transactions full of curious researches and criticisms. These transactions are already highly thought of abroad. One could only wish that some matters had been gone into more deeply and that others had not been treated at all. For example, we could well have done without some dissertation on the prerogatives of the right hand over the left, and a few other researches which under a less silly title are hardly less frivolous.

The Académie des Sciences, in its more difficult and more obviously useful researches, embraces knowledge of nature and the perfection of the arts. It is to be hoped that such profound and sustained studies, such exact calculations, such far-reaching discoveries, such breadth of vision, will at last produce something of benefit to the whole universe.

Until now, as we have already observed together, it has been in the most barbarous times that the most useful discoveries have been made; it seems that the function of the more enlightened periods is to ratiocinate about what ignorant people have invented. We know today, after long disputes between M. Huyghens and M. Renaud, all about determining the most advantageous angle between a ship's rudder and its keel, but Christopher Columbus discovered America without the slightest suspicion of this angle's existence.

I am far from implying from this that we must keep blindly to rule-of-thumb practice, but it would be fortunate if physicists and mathematicians combined as much as possible the practical and the speculative. Is it necessary that what does the greatest honour to the human mind should so often be what is the least useful? A man with the help of the four rules of arithmetic and some common sense becomes a great business man, a Jacques Coeur, a Delmet, a Bernard, whilst some poor algebrist spends his life searching in numbers for relationships and properties, astonishing but quite useless, which won't tell him what the exchange rate is. All the arts are in this kind of situation; there is a point beyond which researches are only for curiosity. These ingenious and useless truths resemble stars which, too far distant from us, give no light.

As for the Académie Française, what a service it would render to literature, the language and the nation if instead of printing compliments year by year it printed the really good works of the age of Louis XIV, cleansed of all the flaws of language that have crept into them! Corneille and Molière are full of them, La Fontaine swarms with them. Those that cannot be corrected might at least be pointed out. Europe, which reads these authors, would learn our language from them with complete confidence, its purity would be fixed for ever; the great French books, printed with this amount of care at the royal expense, would be one of the most glorious monuments of the nation. I have heard that M. Despréaux made this proposal years ago and that it has been repeated by a man whose intelligence, wisdom and balanced critical sense are well known. But this idea has suffered the fate of many other useful projects, namely of being approved and shelved.[46]

*

ON THE *Pensées* OF PASCAL

I AM sending you the critical remarks I have been making for some time on the *Pensées* of M. Pascal. Don't compare me in this matter with Hezekiah, who wanted to burn all the books of Solomon. I respect the genius and the eloquence of Pascal, but the more I respect them the more I am persuaded that he would himself have corrected many of these *Pensées*, which he had jotted down on paper for further examination later. It is while admiring his genius that I challenge some of his ideas.

It seems to me that, in general, the spirit in which Pascal wrote these *Pensées* was to portray man in a hateful light. He is determined to depict us all as evil and unhappy. He writes against human nature more or less as he wrote against the Jesuits.[47] He attributes to the essence of our nature what applies only to certain men. He vilifies the human race eloquently. I venture to champion humanity against this sublime misanthropist; I venture to assert that we are neither so wicked nor so wretched as he says. Moreover, I am quite sure that if in the book he was preparing he had followed the plan indicated in his *Pensées*, he would have produced a book full of eloquent fallacies and admirably argued falsehoods. I even think that all these books written recently to prove the truth of the Christian religion are more calculated to scandalize than edify. Do these writers claim to know more about it than Jesus Christ and the Apostles? It is like seeking to support an oak tree by surrounding it with reeds; you can clear away the reeds without fear of harming the oak.

I have chosen with care some thoughts of Pascal and put the rejoinders after them. It is for you to judge whether I am right or wrong.

1. *The greatnesses and wretchednesses of man are so obvious that it is essential that true religion should teach us that he has within himself some great principle of greatness and at the same time some great principle of wretchedness. For true religion must know our nature intimately, that is to say, know everything that is great and everything that is miserable in it and the reason for each. Furthermore it must explain the amazing contradictions in it.*

This method of reasoning seems false and dangerous, for the fable of Prometheus and Pandora, the hermaphrodites of Plato and the dogmas of the Siamese would equally well justify these apparent contradictions. The Christian religion will remain no less true even if these ingenious conclusions were not drawn from it, which serve no purpose but to shine intellectually.

Christianity only teaches simplicity, humanity and charity. To attempt to reduce it to metaphysics is to turn it into a fount of errors.

2. *Examine in this respect all the religions in the world and see whether any other but Christianity meets the case. Will it be the one taught by the philosophers, who only set before us a conception of good which is in ourselves? Is it the true good? Have they found the cure for our ills? Is it a remedy for the presumption of man to have raised him to the level of God? And have those who have reduced us to the level of animals and given us earthly pleasures as our only good, supplied the remedy for our lusts?*

The philosophers have not taught religion, and there is no point in combating their philosophy. No philosopher has ever claimed to be inspired by God, for had he done so he would have ceased to be a philosopher and acted as a prophet. It is not a matter of knowing whether Christ should triumph over Aristotle, it is a matter of proving that the religion of Christ is the true one, and that those of Mahomet, the Pagans and all the others are false.

3. *And yet without this mystery, the most incomprehensible of all, we are incomprehensible to ourselves. The crux of our condition has its*

twists and turns in the abyss of original sin, so that man is more in-conceivable without this mystery than the mystery is inconceivable to man.

Is it reasoning to say: *Man is inconceivable without this incon-ceivable mystery?* Why seek to go further than Holy Writ? Isn't there some impertinence in believing that Scripture needs support and that these philosophical ideas can give it support?

What would Pascal have replied to a man who said this to him: 'I know that the mystery of original sin is a matter for my faith and not my reason. I understand perfectly well what man is. I see that he comes into the world like the other animals, that childbirth is more painful the more delicate mothers are, that sometimes women and female animals die while giving birth, that sometimes there are defective children who are deprived of one or two senses and of the power of reasoning, that the best organized ones are those who have the strongest passions, that love of self is equal in all men and as necessary to them as the five senses, that this self-love is given us by God for the preservation of our being and that He has given us religion to control this self-love, that our ideas are right or faulty, obscure or luminous according as our organs are more or less healthy, more or less alert, as we are more or less passionate, that we depend for everything on the air surrounding us, on the food we take in, and that in all this there is nothing contradictory. Man is not a puzzle, as you imagine, for the pleasure of solving it. Man seems to be in the right place in nature, superior to the animals, whom he resembles in his organs, inferior to other beings whom he probably resembles by thought. He is, like everything else we behold, a mixture of good and bad, of pleasure and pain. He is provided with passions to make him act, and with reason to govern his acts. If man were perfect he would be God, and these so-called contrarinesses which you call *contradictions*, are the essential ingredients which make up the compound called man, who is what he has to be.'

4. *Let us follow our changes of mood, observe ourselves and see whether we do not find the living characteristics of these two natures.*

Would so many contradictions be found in a simple subject?

This duality of man is so obvious that some people have thought we had two souls, as one simple subject seemed to them incapable of such great and sudden variations from overweening presumption to horrible inner collapse.

Our varied urges are not contradictions in nature and man is not a simple subject. He is composed of an infinite number of organs: if a single one of those organs is at all damaged it must modify all the impressions of the mind, and the animal will have new thoughts and new wishes. It is quite true that sometimes we are overcome with misery and sometimes puffed up with presumption, and that is bound to be so when we find ourselves in quite opposite situations. An animal whom his master caresses and feeds, and another being slowly and skilfully killed for purposes of dissection, experience quite opposite feelings, and so do we, and the differences within us are so far from being contradictory that it would be contradictory if they did not exist.

Fools who have said we have two souls might for the same reason have given us thirty or forty, for a man in the heat of passion often has thirty or forty different ideas of the same thing, and must of necessity have them as this thing appears to him with different aspects.

This supposed dual nature of man is an idea as absurd as it is metaphysical. I might just as well say that a dog who bites and caresses is dual, that a hen who takes so much care of her chicks and then abandons them to the point of repudiating them is dual, that a mirror that reflects different objects at the same time is dual, that a tree sometimes full and sometimes stripped of leaves is dual. I admit that man is incomprehensible, but so is the rest of nature, and there are no more obvious contradictions in man than in the rest.

5. *Not to wager that God exists is to wager that He does not. Which will you take on? Let us weigh the gain and the loss if we decide to believe that God exists. If you win, you win all; if you lose, you lose nothing.*

Therefore wager that He exists, with no hesitation – Yes, I must wager, but perhaps the stakes are too high – Now look, since there is an equal chance of gain or loss, even if you had only two lives to win for one, you could still bet.

It is patently false to say: '*Not to wager that God exists is to wager that He does not*', for the man who doubts and asks to be enlightened certainly does not wager for or against.

Moreover, this article looks somewhat unseemly and puerile; this idea of a gamble, loss or gain, is unsuitable for the solemnity of the subject.

And again, my interest in believing a thing is no proof of the existence of that thing. I will give you sway over the whole world, you say, if I believe you are right. Of course I wish with all my heart that you may be right, but until you have proved it to me I cannot believe you.

Begin, one might say to Pascal, by convincing my reason. It is in my interest, no doubt, that there is a God, but if, in your system, God only came for so few people, if the small number of the elect is so terrifying, if I can do nothing at all by my own efforts, tell me, please, what interest I have in believing you? Have I not an obvious interest in being persuaded to the contrary? How can you have the effrontery to show me an infinite happiness to which hardly one in a million has the right to aspire? If you want to convince me, set about it in some other way, and don't sometimes talk to me about games of chance, wagers and heads or tails, and sometimes frighten me by the thorns you scatter on the path I want to follow and must follow. Your reasoning would only serve to make atheists were it not that the voice of the whole of nature cries out that there is a God with a strength as great as the weakness of these subtleties.

6. *Seeing the blindness and wretchedness of man and the astonishing contradictions to be found in his nature, and looking at the silent universe and man with no light, left to himself and as it were lost in this corner of the universe, not knowing who put him there, what he is supposed to do there, what will become of him when he dies, I go into a panic like a man*

carried asleep to a deserted and terrifying island who wakes up without knowing where he is and with no way of escape. And I marvel that one does not fall into despair at such a miserable state.

As I read this reflection I receive a letter from a friend of mine who lives in a distant country. Here are his words:

'I am living here just as you left me, neither happier nor sadder, nor richer nor poorer, enjoying perfect health, having everything that makes life pleasant, without love, avarice, ambition or desire, and so long as it lasts I shall venture to call myself a very happy man.'

There are plenty of men as happy as he. It is with men as with animals: one dog sleeps and eats with his mistress, another turns a spit and is quite as happy, another goes mad and has to be killed. As for me, when I look at Paris or London I see no reason for falling into this despair Pascal talks about. I see a city not looking in the least like a desert island, but populous, wealthy, policed, where men are as happy as human nature permits. What man of sense will be prepared to hang himself because he doesn't know how one looks upon God face to face, and his reason cannot unravel the mystery of the Trinity? One might just as well despair because one hasn't four legs and a pair of wings.

Why make us feel disgusted with our being? Our existence is not so wretched as we are led to believe. To look on the world as a prison cell and all men as criminals is the idea of a fanatic. To believe that the world is a place of delights in which we can find nothing but enjoyment is the dream of a Sybarite. To think that the world, men and animals are what they have to be in the order of Providence is, I believe, the mark of a sensible man.

7. (*The Jews think*) *that God will not for ever leave the other peoples in darkness, that there will come a deliverer for all men, that they are in the world to announce Him, that they are formed expressly to be heralds of this great event and to call all nations to unite with them in awaiting this deliverer.*

The Jews have always been waiting for a deliverer, but their deliverer is for them and not for us. They are waiting for a Messiah who will make the Jews masters of the Christians, while we hope that the Messiah will one day reunite Jews and Christians. On this they think precisely the opposite of what we do.

8. *The law by which this people is governed is at the same time the oldest, the most perfect and the only law in the world which has always been observed without interruption in a State. This is what Philo, a Jew, shows in several places, and Josephus defends admirably against Apion, where he points out that it is so ancient that the very word law was only known by the most ancient peoples more than a thousand years later, so that Homer, who mentioned so many peoples, never used it. And it is easy to judge of the perfection of this law by simply reading it, when it can be seen that it provides for all things with so much wisdom, equity and good judgement that the most ancient Greek and Roman legislators, having some inkling of it, borrowed their principal laws from it. This can be seen from the ones they call the Twelve Tables, and by other proofs adduced by Josephus.*

It is quite untrue that the law of the Jews is the oldest, since before their legislator Moses they lived in Egypt, the most renowned land in all the world for its wise laws.

It is quite untrue that the word law was unknown until after Homer. He mentions the laws of Minos; the word law is in Hesiod. And even if the word law were neither in Hesiod nor in Homer, it would prove nothing. There were Kings and Judges, so there were laws.

Furthermore it is quite untrue that the Greeks and Romans took over Jewish laws. That cannot have been in the early days of their republics because at that time they could not have known of the Jews; it cannot be in the time of their greatness because then they had for these barbarians a contempt known throughout the world.

9. *This nation is moreover admirable in its integrity. The people keep with love and faith the book in which Moses declares that they hav*

126

always been without gratitude towards God, and that he knows they will be even more so after his death, but that he calls heaven and earth to witness that he has told them enough; that at last God, angered against them, will disperse them among all the peoples of the earth; that as they have angered Him by worshipping Gods who were not their Gods, so He will anger them by calling a people who were not His people. Yet they preserve at the cost of their lives this book that dishonours them in so many ways. This is an integrity without parallel in the world or origin in nature.

There are examples of this integrity everywhere, and its roots are in nature alone. The pride of every Jew has an interest in believing that it is not his detestable politics, his ignorance of the arts, his vulgarity that have been his undoing, but the anger of God punishing him. He thinks with self-satisfaction that miracles were needed to strike him down, and that his nation is still the favourite of God who is chastening it.

Let a preacher mount into the pulpit and say to the French: 'You are despicable, with neither courage nor morals. You were beaten at Hochstadt and Ramillies because you couldn't defend yourselves' – he will be stoned to death. But if he says: 'You are Catholics beloved of God, your wicked sins had angered the Lord, who delivered you up to the heretics at Hochstadt and Ramillies, but when you returned to the Lord He poured His blessing on your courage at Denain' – these words will earn him the love of his audience.

10. *If there is a God we must love Him alone, and not created things.*

We must love all creatures with all our hearts; we must love country, wife, father, children; and we must love them so well that God helps us to love them in spite of ourselves. The opposite principles can only produce barbarous reasoners.

11. *We are born unjust, for each of us is out for himself. That is against all order. We should work for the general good, and the tendency towards self-interest is the beginning of all disorder, in warfare, government, economy,* etc.

That is perfectly in order. It is as impossible for a society to be formed and be durable without self-interest as it would be to produce children without carnal desire or to think of eating without appetite, etc. It is love of self that encourages love of others, it is through our mutual needs that we are useful to the human race. That is the foundation of all commerce, the eternal link between men. Without it not a single art would have been invented, no society of ten people formed. It is this self-love, that every animal has received from nature, which warns us to respect that of others. The law controls this self-love and religion perfects it. It is quite true that God might have created beings solely concerned with the good of others. In that case merchants would have gone to the Indies out of charity and the mason would have cut stone to give pleasure to his neighbour. But God has ordained things differently. Let us not condemn the instinct He has given us, and let us put it to the use He commands.

12. (*The hidden meaning of the Prophecies*) *could not lead into error, and only a people as fleshly as they could make any mistake about it. For when riches are promised in abundance, what prevented their understanding true wealth except their cupidity, which applied this meaning to the good things of the world?*

In all good faith, would even the most spiritual people in the world have understood it in any other way? They were slaves of the Romans, they were awaiting a deliverer who would bring them victory and give Jerusalem the respect of the world. How given the light of their reason, could they see this conqueror this monarch in Jesus, a poor man crucified? How could these people, to whom the *Decalogue* had not even mentioned the immortality of the soul, envisage from the name of their capital a heavenly Jerusalem? How, without some higher guidance could a people so attached to the law recognize in the prophecies, which were not their law, a God hidden in the person of a circumcised Jew who, with his new religion, destroyed and rendered abominable both circumcision and the Sabbath, the sacred foundations of Hebrew law? Had Pascal been born among the Jews, he would have made the same error. Once again, let us worship God without attempting to pierce the obscurity of His mysteries.

13. The time of the first coming of Jesus Christ is foretold. The time of the second is not, because the first was to be hidden, whereas the second is to be in a blaze of light and so manifest that even His enemies will recognize it.

The time of the second coming of Christ has been foretold even more clearly than the first. Pascal had apparently forgotten that in the 21st chapter of St Luke Jesus says expressly:

And when ye shall see Jerusalem compassed with armies, then know that the desolation thereof is nigh . . . and Jerusalem shall be trodden down . . . and there shall be signs in the sun, and in the moon, and in the stars . . . the sea and the waves roaring . . . for the powers of heaven shall be shaken, and then shall they see the Son of Man coming in a cloud with power and great glory.'

Is that not the second coming foretold distinctly? But if it has not yet happened, it is not for us to question Providence.

14. The Messiah, according to the carnally minded Jews, is to be a great temporal prince. For carnally minded Christians He has come to exempt us from loving God and to give us sacraments that do all the work without us. Neither of these is the Christian or the Jewish religion.

This article is more a piece of satire than a Christian reflection. It is clearly the Jesuits who are the target here. But in reality has any Jesuit ever said that Jesus Christ *came to exempt us from loving God?* The dispute about the love of God is a pure dispute of words, like most other scientific quarrels which have given rise to such bitter hatreds and horrible miseries.

There is yet another flaw in this article. It is that it supposes that the expectation of a Messiah was a matter of faith for the Jews. It was merely a consoling thought widely held in this nation. The Jews hoped for a liberator. But they were not ordered to believe this as an act of faith. The whole of their religion was contained in the books of the law. The Prophets were never regarded by the Jews as legislators.

15. *In order to examine the Prophecies they must be understood. For if it is believed that they have only one meaning, it is certain that the Messiah has not yet come. But if they have a double meaning it is certain that he has come in the person of Jesus Christ.*

The Christian religion is so true that it has no need of dubious proofs. Now if anything could shake the foundations of this holy and reasonable religion, it is this view of Pascal. He wants everything in the Scriptures to have a double meaning; but a man who had the misfortune to be an unbeliever could say to him: He who gives two meanings to his words wants to deceive people, and this duplicity is always punished by law. How then can you unblushingly allow in God what is punishable and hateful in men? And what is more, with what scorn and indignation you treat the pagan oracles because they had double meanings! Could we not rather say that the Prophecies which bear directly on Christ have one meaning only, like those of Daniel, Micah and others? Could we not even say that if we had no knowledge of the Prophecies, religion would be no less proven?

16. *The infinite distance from bodies to spirits represents the infinitely more infinite distance from spirits to charity, for it is supernatural.*

It is to be hoped that Pascal would not have employed this gibberish in his book if he had had the time to write it.

17. *The most obvious weaknesses are strengths to those who take things in the right way. For example, the two genealogies of St Matthew and St Luke. It is clear that there has been no collusion here.*

Should the publishers of the *Pensées* of Pascal have printed this *Pensée*, the mere exposition of which is perhaps capable of being harmful to religion? What is the use of saying that these genealogies, these fundamental points of the Christian faith, contradict each other, without saying in what ways they might agree? He ought to have given the antidote with the poison. What would people think of a lawyer who said: 'My client contradicts himself, but this weakness is a strength for those who know how to take things properly.'?

8. *Let us no longer be blamed for lack of clarity, since that is what we lay claim to. Rather let the truth of religion be recognized in its very obscurity, in the little light we possess on the subject and our indifference towards an understanding of it.*

What strange signs of truth Pascal produces! What other signs has a lie got, then? In order to be believed, it would suffice to say: *I am obscure, I am unintelligible*! It would be more sensible to present to our eyes only the light of faith instead of these obscurities of erudition.

9. *If there were only one religion God would be too easy to see.*

What! You say that if there were only one religion God would be too easy to see! Well, are you forgetting that on each page you are saying that one day there will be only one religion? So according to you God will then be too easy to see.

20. *I say that the Jewish religion consisted in none of these things, but solely in the love of God, and that God disapproved of everything else.*

What! Would God disapprove of everything He himself prescribed so carefully to the Jews, and in such prodigious detail! Is it not true to say that the law of Moses consisted in both love and forms of worship? To reduce everything to the love of God smacks less, perhaps, of the love of God than of the hatred every Jansenist has for his Molinist neighbour.

21. *The most important thing in life is choice of a career, and chance settles that. Custom makes masons, soldiers, roofers.*

What then can determine soldiers, masons and all mechanical workers if not what is called chance and custom? Only in the case of inborn genius can one determine a career for oneself. But for jobs that anybody can do it is perfectly natural and reasonable that custom settles them.

22. *Let any man examine his thoughts and he will find them always concerned with the past and the future. We hardly ever think about the present, and if we do it is only to get guidance from it for shaping the future. The present is never our aim; the past and present are our means, the future alone is our object.*

Far from complaining, we should thank the Author of nature for giving us this instinct that constantly carries us on to the future. Man's most precious treasure is this hope which softens our sufferings and depicts pleasures for us in the future in terms of those we possess at present. If men were unfortunate enough to be concerned only with the present, they would not sow, they would not build, they would not plant or provide for anything, and in the midst of this false enjoyment they would lack everything. Could an intellect like Pascal's run into such a false commonplace as that? Nature has ordained that every man should enjoy the present while feeding himself, procreating children, listening to pleasant sounds, using his powers of thought and feeling, and that on emerging from these states, often in the middle of them, he should think of the morrow; otherwise he would be dying of misery today.

23. *But when I looked closer I found that this distaste men have for repose and staying within themselves comes from a very real cause, which is the natural misery of our weak and mortal condition, so wretched that nothing can console us, when there is nothing to prevent us from thinking about it and we see nothing but ourselves.*

This expression *see nothing but ourselves* makes no sense.

What would a man be like who never did anything and is supposed to contemplate himself? Not only do I say that this man would be an imbecile and useless to society, but I say that his man cannot exist: for what would he contemplate? His body, his feet, his hands, his five senses? Either he would be an idiot or he would make use of all these things. Would that leave only his power of thought to be contemplated? But he cannot contemplate this power except by exercising it. Either he will think of nothing or he will think about ideas he has already had, or he will form new ones. Now ideas can only come from outside, so he is necessarily occupied either with his senses or his ideas. Hence he is either outside himself or an imbecile.

Once again, it is impossible for nature to remain in this imaginary numbness; it is absurd to think so and senseless to aim at it. Man is born for action, as fire tends to rise and a stone to sink. Not to be occupied and not to exist is the same thing for man. The whole difference lies in the occupations being gentle or fierce, dangerous or useful.

4. *Men have a hidden instinct prompting them to seek distraction and occupation with external things, which comes from the consciousness of their continual misery, and they have another hidden instinct, a legacy from the greatness of their primitive nature, which tells them that real happiness can only be found in stillness.*

This hidden instinct being the first principle and necessary foundation of social life, it comes more probably from the goodness of God and it is rather an instrument of our happiness than the consciousness of our misery. I don't know what our first parents did in the earthly paradise, but if each one had thought only of himself the existence of the human race was hazardous indeed. Is it not absurd to think that they had perfect senses, that is to say perfect instruments for action, solely for contemplation? Is it not diverting that thinking brains can imagine that idleness is evidence of greatness and action is evidence of a debasement of our nature?

5. *That is why when Cineas told Pyrrhus, who was proposing to relax with his friends after he had conquered a large part of the world, that he*

would do better to expedite his own happiness by enjoying his rest at onc
without going out to find it at the cost of so many fatigues, he gave hin
advice fraught with great difficulties and scarcely more reasonable tha
the aim of that ambitious young man. Both supposed that man could b
satisfied with himself and his present possessions without filling the voi
of his heart with imaginary hopes, which is untrue. Pyrrhus could no
be happy either before or after conquering the world.

The example of Cineas is good in Boileau's satires, but no
in a philosophical treatise. A wise king can be happy in his ow
place, and the fact that Pyrrhus was depicted as a fool prove
nothing for the rest of mankind.

26. *It must be admitted that man is so unhappy that he would be bore*
even with no external cause for boredom, through his actual condition.

On the contrary, man is so happy in this respect and we ar
so much indebted to the Author of nature for having couple
boredom with inaction in order thereby to force us to be usefu
to our fellow men and to ourselves.

27. *How comes it that this man who has recently lost his only son an*
who, weighed down with lawsuits and disputes, was so distressed th
very morning, has now stopped thinking about it? Do not be surprised
he is wholly taken up with wondering how a stag that his hounds ha
been hotly pursuing for six hours will get away. However full of gri
he may be, man needs no more than this. If you can prevail on him to ,
in for some distraction he is happy for that length of time.

This man is very sensible indeed. Distraction is a more ce
tain cure for grief than quinine for a fever. Let us not blam
nature for this, she is always ready to help us.

28. *Imagine a number of men in chains and all condemned to deat*
some of whom are killed each day in sight of the others. Those who rema
see their own condition in that of their fellows and, looking at each oth
with grief and without hope, wait their turn. That is a picture of t
condition of mankind.

This comparison is certainly not fair: poor wretches in chains being killed one after another are unhappy not only because they suffer, but also because they are experiencing what other men are not suffering. The natural lot of a man is neither to be chained nor killed. On the contrary, all men are made, like the animals and plants, to grow, live a certain time, reproduce and die. In a satire you can show man's bad side as much as you like, but only a moment's thought will make you admit that of all the animals man is the most perfect, the happiest and the longest lived. So that instead of being astonished and self-pitying about the unhappiness and the brevity of life, we should be astonished and thankful for our happiness and its duration. Speaking simply as a philosopher, I venture to say that there is a great deal of pride and temerity in claiming that because of our nature we should be better than we are.

29. *The wisest of the Pagans who said that there is only one God were persecuted, the Jews were hated, the Christians still more.*

They have sometimes been persecuted just as in our own day a man would be who came and preached the worship of a God outside the accepted creed. Socrates was not condemned for saying: *There is only one God,* but for having stood out against the external form of worship of the country and for having most inopportunely made some powerful enemies. Regarding the Jews, they were hated not because they believed in only one God, but because they hated other nations to an absurd degree, because they were barbarians who pitilessly massacred their defeated enemies, because this paltry nation, superstitious, ignorant, with no art and no commerce, looked down on the most civilized peoples. As for the Christians, they were hated by the Pagans because they strove to bring down religion and, the Empire and finally succeeded, just as the Protestants have made themselves the masters in the very countries where for long they were hated, persecuted and massacred.

30. *Montaigne's defects are great. He is full of lewd and improper*

words. This is thoroughly bad. His sentiments about suicide and death are horrible.

Montaigne is speaking as a philosopher, not as a Christian, and he is stating the pros and cons of suicide. Philosophically speaking, what harm does a man do society by leaving it when he is of no further use to it? An old man who suffers unbearable agonies with the stone is told: 'If you don't have it cut out you will die, if you do you may dodder on, dribble and drag about for another year, a burden to yourself and everybody else.' I presume that the old man decides to cease being a burden to anybody: that is roughly the case Montaigne sets out.

31. *How many stars, which did not exist for our earlier scientists, have telescopes revealed to us? The Scriptures used to be attacked because in so many places there is reference to the great number of stars. 'There are only one thousand and twenty-two,' it was said; 'we know that.'*

It is certain that Holy Writ in scientific matters has always accommodated itself to accepted notions. Thus it supposes that the earth is immobile, the sun moves, etc. By no means because of refinements in astronomy does it say that the stars are numberless, but to fit in with popular ideas. In fact, although our eyes only make out about one thousand and twenty-two stars, yet when we look at the sky fixedly our dazzled sight seems to see an infinite number. So Scripture is adopting this popular prejudice, for Scripture was not vouchsafed us to make us into physicists, and there is every likelihood that God did not reveal to Habakkuk, Baruch or Micah that one day an Englishman named Flamsteed[48] would catalogue more than seven thousand stars seen through his telescope.

32. *Is it courage in a dying man to go in weakness and agony to brave an all-powerful and eternal God?*

That has never happened and it could only be in a violent brainstorm that a man could say: 'I believe in God and I defy him!'

33. I am very ready to believe stories for which witnesses go to their deaths.

The difficulty is not only knowing whether one will believe witnesses who die to defend their testimony, as so many fanatics have done, but whether these witnesses really did die for that, whether their testimonies have been preserved, whether they inhabited the countries in which they are said to have died. Why did Josephus, born at about the time of Christ's death, enemy of Herod, not very attached to Judaism, never mention a word about it? That is what Pascal might have worked out with success, as so many eloquent writers have since then.

34. The sciences have two extreme boundaries which meet. The first is the pure natural ignorance in which all men are at birth. The other is the one reached by great souls who, having worked through everything men can know, find they know nothing and find themselves once again in the ignorance from which they set out.

This thought is a pure sophism, and the falsity consists in this word *ignorance*, used with two different meanings. A person who cannot read or write is ignorant, but a mathematician, because he is ignorant of the principles hidden in nature, is not at the degree of ignorance from which he set out when he began to learn to read. Newton did not know why a man can move his arm when he wants to, but he was nonetheless learned about everything else. A man who does not know Hebrew but does know Latin is learned compared with one who only knows French.

35. To be capable of being amused by diversions is not to be happy, for these things come from elsewhere and outside. So they are dependent on and consequently liable to be upset by a thousand happenings which bring inevitable afflictions.

That man is in fact happy who is enjoying himself, and enjoyment can only come from outside. We cannot receive sensations or ideas except through external objects, as we can only feed our bodies by bringing into them foreign substances which turn into our own bodies.

36. *Extreme intelligence is accused of madness, like extreme lack of it. Nothing passes for good except mediocrity.*

It is not extreme intelligence that is accused of madness, but extreme liveliness and volubility of mind. Extreme intelligence is extreme rightness, extreme subtlety, extreme breadth, the diametrical opposite of madness.

Extreme lack of intelligence is a lack of perception, a vacuum of ideas, not madness but stupidity. Madness is a disorganization of the faculties that makes a person see several things too fast or limits the imagination to one single object with excessive application and violence. Neither does mediocrity pass for good, but rather distance from two opposite vices, what is called *the middle way* and not *mediocrity*.

37. *If our condition were really happy, we should not have to avoid thinking about it.*

Our condition is precisely to think about outside things, with which we have a necessary connection. It is wrong to say that a man can be distracted from thinking about the human condition, for whatever he applies his mind to, he applies it to something necessarily connected with the human condition; and once again, to think about oneself, apart from all natural things, is to think about nothing at all unless one is very careful.

Far from preventing a man from thinking of his condition, people never talk to him except about the pleasant side of it. They talk to a scientist about reputation and science, to a prince about matters connected with his greatness, and to everybody about pleasure.

38. *The great and the lowly are subject to the same accidents, same vexations, same passions. But the former are at the top of the wheel and the others near the centre, and thus less disturbed by the same movements.*

It is not true that the lowly feel less keenly than the great;

on the contrary their despairs are more acute because they have fewer resources. Out of a hundred people who kill themselves in London ninety-nine belong to the lower classes and barely one to a higher station. The comparison with the wheel is ingenious and false.

39. *Men cannot be taught to be decent citizens, but they are taught everything else; yet they pride themselves on that more than anything else. Thus they only pride themselves on knowing the one thing they cannot learn.*

Men are taught to be decent citizens. Were it not the case, few people would end up by being so. Let your son as a young child take anything that comes to hand and at fifteen he will be a highway robber; praise him for having told a lie and he will become a false witness; flatter his desires and he will end up for certain as a debauchee. Men are taught everything, virtue, religion.

40. *What a foolish project of Montaigne to portray himself! And to do so not by the way and against his own principles, for all of us fall short sometimes, but acting according to his principles and with a prime and main design. For saying silly things by chance or weakness is an ordinary complaint, but to say them deliberately cannot be tolerated, and especially such things as those.*

What a delightful design Montaigne had to portray himself without artifice as he did! For he has portrayed human nature itself. And what a paltry project of Nicole, Malebranche and Pascal, to belittle Montaigne!

41. *When I have wondered why people have such faith in so many quacks who say they have cures, often to the extent of putting their lives into their hands, it has seemed to me that the real reason is that there are real cures, for it would not be possible for there to be so many bogus ones so generally believed in if none were genuine. If there had been none and all sickness had been incurable, it is impossible that men could have imagined they could believe in them, and what is more that so many others*

could have believed in those who boasted they possessed cures. Similarly if a man boasted he could prevent death, nobody would believe him because there is no example of such a thing. But as there have been very many remedies found genuine to the knowledge of even the greatest men, this has influenced people's credulity because, the thing not being refutable as a general rule (as there are genuine isolated cases), ordinary people, unable to discern which of these cases are genuine, believe in them all. In the same way, what lends credibility to so many alleged effects of the moon is that there are genuine ones, like the tides of the sea.

Thus it also seems clear to me that there are so many bogus miracles, false revelations and pieces of sorcery only because genuine ones do exist.

It seems to me that human nature has no need of the truth in order to fall into falsehood. A thousand false influences were attributed to the moon before anyone imagined the slightest real connection with the tides of the sea. The first man to be ill had no difficulty in believing the first charlatan. Nobody has set eyes on werewolves or sorcerers, but many have believed in them. Nobody has seen the transmutation of metals, but many have been ruined by believing in the philosopher's stone. Did the Romans, the Greeks and all the Pagans only believe in the false miracles with which they were inundated because they had seen genuine ones?

42. *The harbour guides the men on a ship, but where shall we find this guidance in morals?*

In this simple maxim alone, that all nations accept: 'Do as you would be done by.'

43. Ferox gens nullam esse vitam sine armis putat. *They prefer death to peace; others prefer death to war. Any belief may be preferred to life, although love of it seems to be so strong and so natural.*

Tacitus said that of the Catalans, but there is no people of whom it has been said or been possible to say: 'It prefers death to war.'

44. *In proportion as one has more intelligence oneself, one finds there are more original men. Common people see no difference between men.*

There are very few really original men; almost all men order their lives, think and feel under the influence of custom and upbringing. Nothing is so rare as a mind moving along a new route. But among this crowd of men going the same way each one has little differences in gait, which penetrating minds discern.

45. *So there are two types of minds, one penetrates rapidly and in depth the consequences of principles, and that is the intuitive mind; the other comprehends a large number of principles without confusing them, and that is the mathematical mind.*

Nowadays custom, I think, demands that we call mathematical a mind that is methodical and consistent.

46. *Death is easier to endure if you don't think about it than the thought of death when there is no danger of it.*

It cannot be said that a man endures death easily or uneasily when he doesn't think about it at all. He who feels nothing endures nothing.

47. *We suppose that all men conceive and feel in the same way such objects as present themselves, but we suppose this quite gratuitously, for we have not the slightest proof. I realize that the same words are applied to the same circumstances, and that each time a couple of men see, for example, snow, they both describe the appearance of this same object by the same words, both saying that it is white; and from this identity of application people derive a strong conjecture that the thought is identical. But that is not absolutely convincing, though there are grounds for wagering on the affirmative.*

The colour white was not the one to produce as a proof. White, which is a mixture of all the rays, seems brilliant to everybody, dazzles somewhat after a time, produces the same effect on all eyes, but it might be said that the other colours are not perceived by all eyes in the same manner.

48. *All our reasoning boils down to giving in to our emotions.*

Our reasoning boils down to giving in to our emotions in matters of taste, not in matters of science.

49. *Those who judge a work by the rules are to the others as those who possess a watch are to those who do not. One man says: 'We've been here two hours,' another says: 'Only three-quarters of an hour.' I look at my watch and say to the one: 'You are bored,' and to the other: 'Time doesn't hang on your hands.'*

In works of art, music, poetry, painting, it is taste that takes the place of the watch, and a person who judges them only by rules misjudges them.

50. *Caesar was too old, I think, to amuse himself by going off to conquer the world. This amusement was fit for Alexander: he was a young man difficult to stop, but Caesar must have been more mature.*

It is usually imagined that Alexander and Caesar went forth with the object of conquering the world. It is not like that at all. Alexander succeeded Philip in the rank of general of Greece and was charged with the legitimate enterprise of avenging the Greeks for the affronts of the King of Persia; he defeated the common enemy and pushed his conquests as far as India because the kingdom of Darius extended as far as India, just as the Duke of Marlborough would have reached Lyons had it not been for Marshal de Villars.

As for Caesar, he was one of the leaders of the Republic. He quarrelled with Pompey like the Jansenists with the Molinists, and then it was war to the death. A single battle in which fewer than ten thousand men were killed decided everything.

Moreover the *Pensée* of Pascal is perhaps untrue in every sense. Caesar had to be mature in order to thread his way through so much intrigue, and it is astonishing that Alexander, at his age, renounced all pleasure in order to wage such an arduous war.

51. *It is a diverting thought that there are people in the world who, having repudiated all the laws of God and nature, have made laws for themselves which they obey strictly, as for example robbers, etc.*

That is more useful even than diverting to consider, for it proves that no human society can endure for a single day without rules.

52. *Man is neither angel nor brute, and the pity of it is that he who wants to play the angel acts the brute.*

Anyone who seeks to destroy the passions instead of controlling them is trying to play the angel.

53. *A horse does not want to be admired by its fellow. Of course you can see a kind of emulation between them when racing, but that is of no consequence, for back in the stable the heavier and less shapely one doesn't give up his oats to the other because of that. It is not so with men: their virtue is not satisfied with itself, and they are not content unless they get some advantage from it over others.*

The most puny man doesn't give up his bread to someone else, but the stronger takes it away from the weaker; and with animals as with men, the big devour the little.

54. *If man began by studying himself he would see how incapable he is of transcending himself. How could it be that a part should understand the whole? He will perhaps aspire to understand at least the parts with which he is in harmony. But the parts of the world all have such connection and interaction with each other that I think it is impossible to know one without the other and without the whole.*

One should not discourage man from seeking what is useful to him by this reflection that he cannot know everything.

> Non possis oculo quantum contendere Lynceus,
> Non tamen idcirco contemnas lippus inungi.

We know many truths and we have discovered many useful inventions. Let us console ourselves for not knowing possible connections between a spider and the ring of Saturn and continue examining what is within our reach.

55. *If lightning struck low-lying places, poets and those who can only reason about things of that nature would be without proofs.*

A simile is no proof either in poetry or in prose: in poetry it acts as an embellishment, and in prose to illumine and make things easier to appreciate. The poets who have compared the woes of the great to the lightning that strikes the mountain-tops would make opposite comparisons if the opposite happened.

56. *It is this compound of mind and body which has made almost all philosophers confuse notions of things and attribute to the body what can only belong to the mind and to the mind what is only applicable to the body.*

If we knew what mind is, we could complain that philosophers have attributed to it things that it is not concerned with. But we do not understand either mind or body; we have no conception of the one and only very imperfect ideas of the other. So we cannot know what their limits are.

57. *As one says* poetic beauty *one should also say* geometrical *and* medical beauty. *Yet one does not, and the reason is that one knows perfectly well what the object of geometry is and the object of medicine, but one does not know what the agreeable sensation consists of which is the object of poetry. One has no idea what the natural model is that should be imitated, and for want of this knowledge one has invented certain strange terms*: siècle d'or, merveille de nos jours, fatal laurier, bel astre, etc., *and this jargon is called poetic beauty. But any-one who imagines a woman clad on this model will see a pretty young lady all decked out with mirrors and brass chains.*

That is quite false; one does not say *geometrical beauty* or *medical beauty* because a theorem and a purge do not affect the senses pleasantly, and one only applies the word *beauty* to things that charm the senses, such as music, painting, eloquence, poetry, formal architecture, etc.

The reason adduced by Pascal is equally false. We know perfectly well what the object of poetry consists of; it consists of painting with vigour, clarity, delicacy and harmony. Poetry is harmonious eloquence. Pascal must have had very little taste to say that *fatal laurier*, *bel astre* and other sillinesses are poetic beauties, and the editors of these *Pensées* must have been people very ill versed in literature to print a reflection so unworthy of its illustrious author.

I am not sending you my other remarks on the *Pensées* of Pascal, which would involve too long-drawn-out discussions. It suffices to have tried to perceive a few errors of inattention in this great genius, and it is a consolation for an intelligence as limited as mine to be of the opinion that the greatest men do make mistakes like the common herd.

NOTES

THESE notes are necessarily selective. Names of more or less universally known figures are omitted, as are names in one or two lists of worthless and now virtually unknown people whom Voltaire mentions simply for that reason. Such can usually be found in encyclopaedias, the *Dictionary of National Biography* or the biographical section at the end of the Petit Larousse French dictionary.

LETTER 1

1. Matthew 3, 11. Slightly different versions in the other three Gospels.
2. I Corinthians, 1, 17.

LETTER 2

3. Malebranche, Nicolas (1638–1715). Theologian and philosopher, combined close reasoning with visionary mysticism. Involved in much controversy with both the Jansenists and Bossuet.

LETTER 3

4. Fox, George (1624–91). Founder of the Society of Friends. The early Quaker movement was a double reaction, against the 'hireling ministry' and paid hierarchy of the established Church, and also the depressing Calvinist dogma of predestination which condemns most of mankind to eternal damnation through no fault of their own.
5. Barclay, Robert (1648–90). The first Quaker intellectual, his *Apology for the True Christian Divinity* (1678) is a classic of Quakerism.

LETTER 4

6. Penn, Sir William (1621–70). British Admiral, close friend of the

Duke of York, later James II. As a high-ranking naval official he is frequently mentioned in Pepys's Diary.

7. Penn, William (1644–1718). Son of the above, one of the founding fathers of Quakerism. Was granted the ownership of the American region named after him as Pennsylvania. He governed the country wisely and with paternal kindness, and many of his measures have passed into the United States system. Like many Quakers since his time, he combined his religious life with great business success. Voltaire's story is substantially correct.

8. A curious error. Pennsylvania is, of course, north of Maryland.

9. Harley, Robert, Earl of Oxford (1661–1724). Tory politician under Queen Anne. Posterity owes him the Harleian Collection in the British Museum.

10. Bolingbroke, Henry St John, Viscount (1678–1751). English statesman, associate of Harley. For intriguing in the Jacobite cause he was exiled by George I and lived in style in France, not returning until after he was pardoned in 1723. The young Voltaire was a frequent guest at his home in France and owes much of his interest in England, information and opinions to him.

11. Clarke, Samuel (1675–1729). English philosopher and theologian. The two books referred to are: *A Discourse concerning the Being and Attributes of God* (1705) and *The Verity and Certitude of Natural and Revealed Religion* (?1705). His scientific work is equally important. A friend of Newton, he did a Latin translation of his *Opticks*.

12. Voltaire telescopes the Provisions of Oxford (Henry III) and Magna Carta (John).

13. Lady Mary Wortley Montagu (1689–1762). Colourful intel-

lectual and society figure whose husband, Edward Wortley
Montagu, was ambassador to Constantinople 1716–18. Her
Letters on Oriental life were important and influential. Friend of
Addison, Pope and many other literary men.

LETTER 12

14. Thou, Jacques Auguste de (1553–1617). Published an immense
Latin *Historia sui temporis*, part of which was translated into
French by du Ryer in 1659. The complete work was not
published until 1734.

15. Parkins refers to Perkin Warbeck. His cause was backed by the
Duchess of Burgundy, who also protected Lambert Simnel.

LETTER 13

16. Mabillon, Jean (1632–1707). Benedictine monk. Here Voltaire
refers to his *Traité des études monastiques*.

17. Despréaux. Boileau's full name was Nicolas Boileau-Despréaux.
Voltaire uses one or other name indiscriminately.

18. Stillingfleet, Edward (1635–99). English divine, Dean of St
Paul's and Bishop of Worcester. Carried on a polemic of pam-
phlets with Locke in defence of the Trinity against what he
took to be Locke's denial of substance.

19. Voltaire here lumps together thinkers who have held un-
orthodox but not necessarily atheistic views about religion.

LETTER 14

20. Fontenelle, Bernard le Bovier de (1657–1757). Nephew of
Corneille, began his literary career as a fashionable writer of
trivial verse, but soon became interested in science. *Entretiens
sur la Pluralité des Mondes*, a gracefully written popularization of
astronomy and relativity, is his most successful work. He became
Perpetual Secretary of the Académie des Sciences in 1697, was
a member of the London Royal Society, and for most of his
long life occupied a unique position as a popularizer of science
and a kind of liaison officer between scientists from all over
Europe.

21. Picard, Jean (1620–82). French astronomer, one of the first to measure the earth accurately.

22. Bernoulli, Jacques (1654–1705). One of a family of Swiss scientists and mathematicians. Professor of Mathematics in the University of Basel.

23. Whiston, William (1667–1752). Clergyman and mathematician, succeeded Newton in 1703 as Professor of Mathematics in the University of Cambridge, but was deprived in 1710 on account of his Arian views and ultimately became a Baptist. Translated Josephus.

24. Saurin, Joseph (1655–1737). French mathematician. The reference is to *Examen d'une difficulté considérable proposée par M. Huyghens contre le système cartésien sur la cause de la pesanteur* (Mémoires de l'Académie des Sciences, 1709).

25. Dominis, Marco Antonio de (1566–1625). Italian ecclesiastic whose stormy career included a feud with the Pope, a stay in England where he became Anglican Dean of Windsor under James I, flight from England and denunciation of the Church of England, return to Rome, where the Inquisition imprisoned him and he died. In 1611, while he was professor at Padua, he published *De Radiis Visus et Lucis in Vitris Perspectivis et Iride*, in which he pointed out for the first time that the rainbow is simply a matter of refraction of light in raindrops.

26. Brouncker, William, Viscount (1620–84). Anglo-Irish mathematician. First President of the Royal Society. Features frequently in the diaries of Pepys and Evelyn.

27. Hipparchus (2nd century B.C.) Greek astronomer. Discovered the precession of the equinoxes and estimated the distances of sun and moon from the earth.

28. Otway, Thomas (1652–85). English dramatist, wrote both

tragedies and comedies from 1675 onwards, and in 1677 translated Racine's *Bérénice* and Molière's *Les Fourberies de Scapin*. His *Venice Preserv'd* (1682) has a permanent place in English dramatic history.

LETTER 19

29. Muralt, Béat Louis de (1665–1749). Swiss traveller and writer. Published *Lettres sur les Français et les Anglais* and *Lettres sur les Voyages* in 1725, and so as French language commentator on England is an immediate predecessor of Voltaire. Praises English institutions at the expense of French.
30. Wycherley, William (1640–1716). *The Plain Dealer* (1677) and *The Country Wife* (1675).

LETTER 20

31. Hervey, John (1696–1743). Lord Hervey of Ickworth, in Suffolk. Whig politician, important in Walpole's administration. As he was born in 1696, two years after Voltaire himself, he was not so very young when Voltaire refers to him. He was friendly with Voltaire in England, and they corresponded long after Voltaire's return to France. See also Appendix.
32. Rochester, John Wilmot, Earl of (1647–80). Poet and notorious rake in the reign of Charles II. His more serious work includes imitations of Horace and some love poetry, but much of his work is witty obscenity. See also Letter 21.

LETTER 21

33. Waller, Edmund (1606–87). One of the greatest of the Restoration poets. Politically a Vicar of Bray: although a member of the Long Parliament he was implicated in a Royalist plot in 1643 and banished to France until 1651. Then he held office under Cromwell (*A Panegyric to my Lord Protector*, 1655) but welcomed the Restoration (*To the King upon His Majesty's Happy Return*, 1660), and contrived to gain favour and office under both régimes. Wrote the beautiful *Go lovely rose*.
34. Saint-Evremond, Charles de (?1614–1703). In 1661 he fled to England upon the discovery of some subversive writings, and

thenceforth lived most of his life in London. One of the earliest French expatriates, hence his knowledge of Waller.

35. Bayle, Pierre (1647–1706). Author of the famous *Dictionnaire Historique et Critique* (1696–7), a vast work sceptical of all received 'authorities', and one of the intellectual foundations of the eighteenth century.

36. Voiture, Vincent (1597–1648). A wit noted for his letters, which were passed round and much admired. A typical *précieux*. By even comparing them Voltaire does less than justice to Waller.

37. Dorset, Roscommon, Buckingham, Halifax. It may be of interest here to give Pope's remark about some of these court poets: (they) 'should be considered as holiday writers, as gentlemen who divert themselves now and then with poetry, rather than as poets'.

LETTER 22

38. *Hudibras*, by Samuel Butler (1612–80), a satirical burlesque on Puritanism which appealed to Charles II would naturally also appeal to Voltaire. Note Voltaire's very wise remarks about the near-impossibility of translating humour.

39. Voltaire is ostensibly only concerned here with Swift's verse. See Introduction for Voltaire's curiously selective treatment of Swift.

40. Satire of Boileau.

LETTER 23

41. *Rhadamisthe et Zénobie*, tragedy by Crébillon the elder (1674–1762). He was Voltaire's greatest rival in this field. The success of Crébillon's efforts to enliven classical tragedy with violent action and terror probably influenced Voltaire's tragedies more than he would care to admit.

42. Racine, Louis (1692–1763), son of Jean Racine. Biographer of his father. Louis Fagon, son of the notorious Fagon, court physician to Louis XIV, held a responsible financial position during the latter part of the reign of Louis XIV and the Regency. Fagon the elder, the doctor, is the classical example of the hidebound medical man, whose faith in such dogmas as cuppings, bleedings and purges probably hastened the deaths of several members of the royal family.

43. Lecouvreur, Adrienne (1692–1730). French actress, died in the same year as Mrs Oldfield, hence Voltaire's contrast. The circumstances of her death, probably by poison, were worked up into a drama by Scribe and Legouvé (1848).

44. Prynne, William (1600–69). Virulent pamphleteer in the Puritan cause, hence his denunciations of stage plays. Voltaire's story is correct as far as it goes, but misleading, as after the pillorying, ear-cutting and imprisonment he survived for over thirty years, changed sides, as so many did at that period of time-servers, sat in Parliament as a Royalist, and a grateful Charles II made him Keeper of the Tower records. So, in his later life, he was very important as a preserver of ancient records.

45. Senesino and Cuzzoni. Italian castrato and soprano respectively. Stars of many of the Handel opera seasons in London in the 1720s and 30s. Handel wrote some of his greatest rôles for them.

LETTER 24

46. Voltaire's suggestion that the Academy might be better employed in 'purifying' the 'flaws' of language of some of the supreme masters of French classical literature is typical of the conceited complacency of the eighteenth century in matters of literacy taste. They thought they had reached perfection and stability for all time. Compare English seventeenth and eighteenth century 'improvements' to Shakespeare.

LETTER 25

47. In the *Lettres Provinciales* (1656–7), the brilliant satire thanks to which for three hundred years the word Jesuit has been used to denote an unscrupulous trickster and the word casuistry to mean specious excuses and self-justifications. It was because Pascal feared that his book might be taken as hostile to Christianity itself that he sought to make amends by writing a great apologia for religion, which he did not live to complete. The *Pensées* are his notes for the great work.

48. Flamsteed, John (1646–1719). The first Astronomer-Royal of England and first to work in Greenwich Observatory from 1676.

APPENDIX

VOLTAIRE'S VERSE TRANSLATIONS

REAL poetry is untranslatable because by its very nature it depends upon *sounds* that exist in one language and in no other. Voltaire is not so foolish as to claim to translate, and indeed he goes out of his way to point out that he has rendered these English passages very freely. The reader can judge how freely by comparing Voltaire's French versions with the passages below.

LETTER 18

> To be, or not to be: that is the question:
> Whether 'tis nobler in the mind to suffer
> The slings and arrows of outrageous fortune,
> Or to take arms against a sea of troubles,
> And by opposing end them. To die: to sleep;
> No more; and by a sleep to say we end
> The heart-ache, and the thousand natural shocks
> That flesh is heir to, 'tis a consummation
> Devoutly to be wish'd. To die, to sleep;
> To sleep: perchance to dream: ay, there's the rub;
> For in that sleep of death what dreams may come,
> When we have shuffled off this mortal coil,
> Must give us pause: there's the respect
> That makes calamity of so long life;
> For who would bear the whips and scorns of time,
> The oppressor's wrong, the proud man's contumely,
> The pangs of despised love, the law's delay,
> The insolence of office, and the spurns
> That patient merit of the unworthy takes,
> When he himself might his quietus make
> With a bare bodkin? Who would fardels bear,
> To grunt and sweat under a weary life,
> But that the dread of something after death,
> The undiscover'd country from whose bourn
> No traveller returns, puzzles the will,
> And makes us rather bear those ills we have
> Than fly to others that we know not of?

Thus conscience does make cowards of us all,
And thus the native hue of resolution
Is sicklied o'er with the pale cast of thought,
And enterprises of great pitch and moment
With this regard their currents turn awry
And lose the name of action. etc.

Hamlet, III, 1

When I consider Life, 'tis all a Cheat,
Yet fool'd by Hope, Men favour the Deceit;
Trust on and think Tomorrow will repay;
Tomorrow's falser than the former Day;
Lies worse; and whilst it says we shall be blest
With some new Joys, cuts off what we possest;
Strange Cozenage! none wou'd live past Years again;
Yet all hope Pleasure in what yet remain,
And from the Dregs of Life think to receive
What the first sprightly Running could not give.
I'm tir'd with waiting for this chymic Gold,
Which fools us young, and beggars us when old.

DRYDEN: *Aureng-Zebe*, IV, 1

LETTER 20

Gustave Lanson, in his great edition of the *Lettres philosophiques*, says not only that he has failed to find the original poem of Lord Hervey of which Voltaire gives his version, but that the English edition of 1733 did not give it either.

LETTER 21

Lanson points out that Voltaire has made a continuous poem out of odd bits of Rochester's *Satire against Man*. Here are the bits:

And 'tis this very Reason I despise . . .
. . . 'Tis not true Reason I despise, but yours.

. . . that vain animal
Who is so proud of being rational . . .
Reason, an *Ignis fatuus* in the Mind . . .

Bless'd, glorious Man to whom alone kind Heav'n
An everlasting soul has freely giv'n;
Whom his great Maker took such care to make,

155

That from himself he did the Image take,
And this fair Frame in shining Reason drest,
To dignify his Nature above beast . . .
(We) Dive into mysteries; then, soaring, pierce
The flaming limits of the Universe.

This supernatural Gift, that makes a mite
Think he's the image of the Infinite . . .

This busie puzzling stirrer up of Doubt
That frames deep Mysteries, then finds 'em out;
Filling with frantic Crowds of thinking Fools,
These rev'rend Bedlams, Colleges and Schools;
Borne on those wings, each heavy sot can pierce
The limits of the boundless Universe . . .

And we have modern cloister'd Coxcombs, who
Retire to think, 'cause they have nought to do:
But thoughts are given for Action's Government;
Where Action ceases, Thought is impertinent.
Our sphere of action is life's happiness;
And he who thinks beyond, thinks like an Ass.

*   *   *

We must resign! Heav'n his great soul does claim
In storms as loud as his immortal Fame:
His dying Groans, his last Breath shakes our Isle,
And Trees uncut fall for his fun'ral pile:
About his Palace their broad roots are tost
Into the air; so Romulus was lost!
New Rome in such a Tempest miss'd her King.
And from obeying fell to worshipping:
On Œta's top thus Hercules lay dead,
With ruin's Oaks and Pines about him spread.
. . . Nature herself took Notice of his death,
And, sighing, swell'd the Sea with such a breath,
That to remotest Shores the billows roul'd,
Th'approaching Fate of his great Ruler told.

WALLER

LETTER 22

This is a good example of the extreme freedom of Voltaire's rendering. The following lines from Pope's *The Rape of the Lock*, Canto IV
correspond only roughly. It will be seen that Voltaire suppressed

some of Pope's material and padded other parts with matter of his own:

> Umbriel, a dusky, melancholy sprite,
> As ever sully'd the fair face of light,
> Down to the central earth, his proper scene,
> Repair'd to search the gloomy Cave of Spleen.
>   Swift on his sooty pinions flits the Gnome,
> And in a vapour reach'd the dismal dome.
> No cheerful breeze this sullen region knows,
> The dreaded East is all the wind that blows.
> Here in a grotto, shelter'd close from air,
> And screen'd in shades from day's detested glare,
> She sighs for ever on her pensive bed,
> Pain at her side, and Megrim at her head.
>   Two handmaids wait the throne: alike in place,
> But diff'ring far in figure and in face.
> Here stood Ill-nature like an ancient maid,
> Her wrinkled form in black and white array'd;
> With store of pray'rs, for mornings, nights, and noons,
> Her hand is fill'd; her bosom with lampoons.
>   There Affectation, with a sickly mien,
> Shows in her cheek the roses of eighteen,
> Practis'd to lisp, and hang the head aside,
> Faints into airs, and languishes with pride,
> On the rich quilt sinks with becoming woe,
> Wrapt in a gown, for sickness, and for show.

MORE ABOUT PENGUINS
AND PELICANS

Penguinews, which appears every month, contains details of all the new books issued by Penguins as they are published. It is supplemented by our stocklist, which includes around 5,000 titles.

A specimen copy of *Penguinews* will be sent to you free on request. Please write to Dept EP, Penguin Books Ltd, Harmondsworth, Middlesex, for your copy.

In the U.S.A.: For a complete list of books available from Penguins in the United States write to Dept CS, Penguin Books, 625 Madison Avenue, New York, New York 10022.

In Canada: For a complete list of books available from Penguins in Canada write to Penguin Books Canada Ltd, 2801 John Street, Markham, Ontario L3R 1B4.

In Australia: For a complete list of books available from Penguins in Australia write to the Marketing Department, Penguin Books Australia Ltd, P.O. Box 257, Ringwood, Victoria 3134.